THE BEST–LOVED POEMS OF

JACQUELINE KENNEDY ONASSIS

Selected and Introduced by

CAROLINE KENNEDY

GⅡC

GRAND CENTRAL
PUBLISHING

NEW YORK   BOSTON

Grand Central Publishing
Hachette Book Group
1290 Avenue of the Americas
New York, NY 10104

www.HachetteBookGroup.com

Printed in the United States of America

RRD-C

Originally published in hardcover by Hyperion
First Grand Central Publishing edition: February 2015

10 9 8 7 6 5 4 3 2 1

Grand Central Publishing is a division of Hachette Book Group, Inc.
The Grand Central Publishing name and logo are trademarks of Hachette Book Group, Inc.

The Hachette Speakers Bureau provides a wide range of authors for speaking events. To find out more, go to www.hachettespeakersbureau.com or call (866) 376-6591.

The publisher is not responsible for websites (or their content) that are not owned by the publisher.

Library of Congress Cataloging-in-Publication Data

The Best-loved poems of Jacqueline Kennedy Onassis / [selected and introduced by Caroline Kennedy].
    p. cm.
    1. Poetry—Collections. I. Onassis, Jacqueline Kennedy, 1929– II. Kennedy, Caroline, 1957–

PN6101 .B39 2001
808.81—dc21   2001024466

ISBN 978-1-4555-9157-2

Book design by Casey Hampton

CONTENTS

FOREWORD *Caroline Kennedy* x i

AMERICA

INTRODUCTION *Caroline Kennedy* 3
AMERICA, THE BEAUTIFUL *Katherine Lee Bates* 7
FOR JOHN F. KENNEDY HIS INAUGURATION
   Robert Frost 9
THE GIFT OUTRIGHT *Robert Frost* 1 2
PAUL REVERE'S RIDE *Henry Wadsworth Longfellow* 1 3
I HEAR AMERICA SINGING *Walt Whitman* 1 8
LET AMERICA BE AMERICA AGAIN *Langston Hughes* 1 9
BROWN RIVER, SMILE *Jean Toomer* 2 3

FIRST POEMS

INTRODUCTION *Caroline Kennedy* 3 1
FIRST FIG *Edna St. Vincent Millay* 3 3

SECOND FIG *Edna St. Vincent Millay* 33

FOG *Carl Sandburg* 34

AT THE ANCIENT POND *Basho* 35

HOW RELUCTANTLY *Basho* 35

THE LAND OF COUNTERPANE *Robert Louis Stevenson* 36

THE SWING *Robert Louis Stevenson* 37

BED IN SUMMER *Robert Louis Stevenson* 38

TEDDY BEAR'S PICNIC *Jimmy Kennedy* 39

THREE PONIES *Arthur Guiterman* 41

THE YAK *Theodore Roethke* 42

GRIZZLY BEAR *Mary Austin* 43

THE ELEPHANT *Hilaire Belloc* 44

THE LITTLE TURTLE *Vachel Lindsay* 45

DOGS AND WEATHER *Winifred Welles* 46

LITTLE TROTTY WAGTAIL *John Clare* 47

THE OWL AND THE PUSSY-CAT *Edward Lear* 48

THE CROCODILE *Lewis Carroll* 50

FIREFLIES IN THE GARDEN *Robert Frost* 51

THE ROSE FAMILY *Robert Frost* 52

WHO HAS SEEN THE WIND? *Christina Rossetti* 53

TARANTELLA *Hilaire Belloc* 54

SHERWOOD *Alfred Noyes* 56

ANNABEL LEE *Edgar Allan Poe* 59

SOME KEEP THE SABBATH GOING TO CHURCH
    Emily Dickinson 61

HOPE IS THE THING WITH FEATHERS *Emily Dickinson* 62

MOTHER TO SON *Langston Hughes* 63

THE RED WHEELBARROW *William Carlos Williams* 64

PSALM 23 65

LUKE 2: 1—14 66

A VISIT FROM ST. NICHOLAS *Clement Clarke Moore* 67

ADVENTURE

INTRODUCTION *Caroline Kennedy* 71

SKYE BOAT SONG 73

CARGOES *John Masefield* 75

SEA-FEVER *John Masefield* 76

HUNTING-SONG OF THE SEEONEE PACK *Rudyard Kipling* 77

TABLEAU *Countee Cullen* 78

MERRY-GO-ROUND *Langston Hughes* 79

THE ROAD NOT TAKEN *Robert Frost* 80

SONG *John Donne* 81

RICHARD III, I, i, 1—13 *William Shakespeare* 82

HENRY V, IV, iii, 40—67 (ST. CRISPIN'S DAY SPEECH)
    William Shakespeare 83

THE ISLES OF GREECE *George Gordon, Lord Byron* 84

ULYSSES *Alfred Lord Tennyson* 88

ITHACA *Constantine P. Cavafy* 91

ESCAPE

INTRODUCTION *Caroline Kennedy* 95

THE FLOWERS *Robert Louis Stevenson* 97

BEHIND STOWE *Elizabeth Bishop* 98

IN JUST *E. E. Cummings* 99

THE PASTURE *Robert Frost* 100

PORTRAIT BY A NEIGHBOUR *Edna St. Vincent Millay* 101

THE SONG OF WANDERING AENGUS *William Butler Yeats* 102

THE LAKE ISLE OF INNISFREE *William Butler Yeats* 103

THE ODYSSEY, BOOK IX *Homer* 104

THE TEMPEST, V, i, 104—110 (ARIEL'S SONG)
    William Shakespeare 105

I TASTE A LIQUOR NEVER BREWED *Emily Dickinson* 106

THESE ARE THE DAYS WHEN BIRDS COME BACK
    Emily Dickinson 107

STOPPING BY WOODS ON A SNOWY EVENING *Robert Frost* 108

KUBLA KHAN *Samuel Taylor Coleridge* 109
THE DAWN *William Butler Yeats* 111
SAILING TO BYZANTIUM *William Butler Yeats* 112
OF MERE BEING *Wallace Stevens* 114

ROMANCE AND LOVE

INTRODUCTION *Caroline Kennedy* 117
THE SONG OF SOLOMON 2: 8—16 119
PARADISE LOST, BOOK IV, 639—658 *John Milton* 120
ROMEO AND JULIET, III, ii, 17—31
   William Shakespeare 121
SONNET XVIII *William Shakespeare* 122
SONNET XXIX *William Shakespeare* 123
SONNET CXVI *William Shakespeare* 124
THE BARGAIN *Sir Philip Sidney* 125
THE PASSIONATE SHEPHERD TO HIS LOVE
   Christopher Marlowe 126
HER REPLY *Sir Walter Raleigh* 127
SHE WALKS IN BEAUTY *George Gordon, Lord Byron* 128
DR. FAUSTUS, SCENE XIII *Christopher Marlowe* 129
THE HILL *Rupert Brooke* 130
THE VASE OF PERFUME *Chang Wu-chien* 131
WHEN A BEGGAR BEHOLDS YOU . . . *Anonymous* 132
SOMEWHERE I HAVE NEVER TRAVELLED, GLADLY BEYOND
   E. E. Cummings 133
FOR C. K. AT HIS CHRISTENING *Daniel Lawrence Kelleher* 134
A PRAYER IN SPRING *Robert Frost* 135
CORINTHIANS 13: 1—13 136

REFLECTION

INTRODUCTION *Caroline Kennedy* 139
ECCLESIASTES 3:1—8 140
PRAYER FOR PEACE *St. Francis of Assisi* 141

SONNET ON HIS BLINDNESS *John Milton* 142

DEATH, BE NOT PROUD *John Donne* 143

OZYMANDIAS *Percy Bysshe Shelley* 144

HIS PILGRIMAGE *Sir Walter Raleigh* 145

ODE ON A GRECIAN URN *John Keats* 146

ANTIGONE, ODE I *Sophocles* 148

AGAMEMNON, ACT I *Aeschylus* 149

OLYMPIAN ODE II *Pindar* 150

MAGPIES IN PICARDY *T. P. Cameron Wilson* 151

AFTERMATH *Siegfried Sassoon* 153

THE SECOND COMING *William Butler Yeats* 155

CHOOSE SOMETHING LIKE A STAR *Robert Frost* 156

ONE ART *Elizabeth Bishop* 157

THE NEGRO SPEAKS OF RIVERS *Langston Hughes* 158

ACQUAINTED WITH THE NIGHT *Robert Frost* 159

THE TRULY GREAT *Stephen Spender* 160

FOR A POET *Countee Cullen* 161

HE WISHES FOR THE CLOTHS OF HEAVEN
   William Butler Yeats 162

MATTHEW 5:1—10 163

IN HER OWN WORDS

INTRODUCTION *Caroline Kennedy* 167

ESSAY *Jacqueline Kennedy Onassis* 168

SEA JOY *Jacqueline Bouvier* 169

THOUGHTS *Jacqueline Bouvier* 170

MEANWHILE IN MASSACHUSETTS
   Jacqueline Bouvier Kennedy 172

ONE OF THE GREATEST GIFTS my brother and I received from my mother was her love of literature and language. In this anthology, I have tried to include poems that reflect things that were important to her—a spirit of adventure, the worlds of imagination and nature, and the strength of love and family. There are poems to read with children, poems for readers just starting out on their own, and poems for those who have never really thought poetry was for them.

Sometimes, knowing that someone else liked a certain poem can cause us to take another look at it, puzzle over why they might have liked it, and before we know it, be captivated by it ourselves. Poems often express what we believe to be our thoughts alone, and poets can become our companions as we journey into new worlds of imagination, feeling, and possibility.

My mother was lucky to have a grandfather who loved poetry. When she was a little girl, she would visit him every Wednesday evening after dancing class, and they would memorize poems together. I feel fortunate that she passed this gift along to John and me, teaching us poems she loved as well as encouraging us to discover poems on our own.

Now that I have my own children, I understand in a new way that if you love something, your children will want to love it too. As parents, we have a chance to help our children go beyond us, and to start them off on a lifelong voyage of discovery and self-discovery. I hope poetry will become part of my children's lives, your life, and then your children's, not only because of the pleasure it will bring, but because the power of ideas, and the ability to express them, is the greatest power we have.

AMERICA

THE IDEA OF AMERICA—freedom, equality, possibility—has been celebrated in poetry, song, political rhetoric, and judicial opinion. The poems that follow serenade America and explore the individual's role in shaping our national destiny. They describe heroes like Paul Revere, the American Everyman about whom Walt Whitman sings, and those who have been shut out of the American dream but whose struggles are given voice by Langston Hughes. These poems remind us that no matter who we are, we each have an opportunity to help create the kind of society we want to live in. For America's story is still unfolding—in the words of Robert Frost, it is our country, "such as she was, such as she will become."

"Paul Revere's Ride" by Henry Wadsworth Longfellow always reminds me of my grandmother, Rose Fitzgerald Kennedy. When I was a child, she was the most patriotic person I knew. At family gatherings, she used to recite this poem from memory and encouraged (with varying degrees of success) her grandchildren

3

to do the same. She was baptized around the corner from the Old North Church and grew up in Concord, Massachusetts. Since she had been born before 1900, to me it was perfectly possible that she might have even caught a glimpse of Paul Revere.

Grandma's recitation of the poem combined patriotism, her Irish antipathy toward the English, her love of language, and her conviction that one man's courage could change the course of history. She instilled in us the belief that perhaps, if the chance came again, we would be the one to inspire others, just like Paul Revere. (Of course, as my daughter recently reminded me, it was really the poet who inspired us since there were two other men who rode that night, William Dawes and Samuel Prescott, whose names are largely forgotten.)

To me, the most meaningful poem in this section is Robert Frost's "The Gift Outright," which the poet recited at my father's inauguration. By asking Frost to read that day, my father expressed his belief in the power of language and connected the inaugural ceremony to an enduring tradition of using poetry, in a sense, to sanctify an occasion.

A snowstorm had blanketed the Capitol the night before, but the morning was glistening bright. When Frost stood to read the poem he had written for the occasion, the glare was so strong he couldn't see the words on the page. He recited "The Gift Outright" from memory. The contrast between his age and my father's youth, the poet's frailty and the power of his words gave the moment a special significance.

Three years later, at the dedication of a library named for Robert Frost, President Kennedy said, "The men who create power

4

make an indispensable contribution to the Nation's greatness, but the men who question power make a contribution just as indispensable, especially when that questioning is disinterested, for they determine whether we use power, or power uses us. . . . When power leads man towards arrogance, poetry reminds him of his limitations. When power narrows the area of man's concern, poetry reminds him of the richness and diversity of his existence. When power corrupts, poetry cleanses. For art establishes the basic human truth which must serve as the touchstone of our judgment."

Throughout her life, my mother took great pride in the role of poetry and the arts in my father's administration. She celebrated American arts and artists in the White House, believing, as my father did, that America's artistic achievements were equal to her political and military power, and that American civilization had come of age.

AMERICA, THE BEAUTIFUL
Katharine Lee Bates

O beautiful for spacious skies,
   For amber waves of grain,
For purple mountain majesties
   Above the fruited plain!
      America! America!
   God shed His grace on thee,
And crown thy good with brotherhood
   From sea to shining sea!

O beautiful for pilgrim feet,
   Whose stern, impassioned stress
A thoroughfare for freedom beat
   Across the wilderness!
      America! America!
   God mend thine every flaw,
Confirm thy soul in self-control,
   Thy liberty in law!

O beautiful for heroes proved
   In liberating strife,
Who more than self their country loved,
   And mercy more than life!
      America! America!
   May God thy gold refine
Till all success be nobleness
   And every gain divine!

O beautiful for patriot dream
   That sees beyond the years

Thine alabaster cities gleam
   Undimmed by human tears!
      America! America!
    God shed His grace on thee
And crown thy good with brotherhood
   From sea to shining sea!

FOR JOHN F. KENNEDY HIS INAUGURATION
Robert Frost

Summoning artists to participate
In the august occasions of the state
Seems something artists ought to celebrate.
Today is for my cause a day of days.
And his be poetry's old-fashioned praise
Who was the first to think of such a thing.
This verse that in acknowledgment I bring
Goes back to the beginning of the end
Of what had been for centuries the trend;
A turning point in modern history.
Colonial had been the thing to be
As long as the great issue was to see
What country'd be the one to dominate
By character, by tongue, by native trait,
The new world Christopher Columbus found.
The French, the Spanish, and the Dutch were downed
And counted out. Heroic deeds were done.
Elizabeth the First and England won.
Now came on a new order of the ages
That in the Latin of our founding sages
(Is it not written on the dollar bill
We carry in our purse and pocket still?)
God nodded his approval of as good.
So much those heroes knew and understood,
I mean the great four, Washington,
John Adams, Jefferson, and Madison,—
So much they knew as consecrated seers
They must have seen ahead what now appears,
They would bring empires down about our ears

And by the example of our Declaration
Make everybody want to be a nation.
And this is no aristocratic joke
At the expense of negligible folk.
We see how seriously the races swarm
In their attempts at sovereignty and form.
They are our wards we think to some extent
For the time being and with their consent,
To teach them how Democracy is meant.
"New order of the ages" did they say?
If it looks none too orderly today,
'Tis a confusion it was ours to start
So in it have to take courageous part.
No one of honest feeling would approve
A ruler who pretended not to love
A turbulence he had the better of.
Everyone knows the glory of the twain
Who gave America the aeroplane
To ride the whirlwind and the hurricane.
Some poor fool has been saying in his heart
Glory is out of date in life and art.
Our venture in revolution and outlawry
Has justified itself in freedom's story
Right down to now in glory upon glory.
Come fresh from an election like the last,
The greatest vote a people ever cast,
So close yet sure to be abided by,
It is no miracle our mood is high.
Courage is in the air in bracing whiffs
Better than all the stalemate an's and ifs.
There was the book of profile tales declaring
For the emboldened politicians daring

To break with followers when in the wrong,
A healthy independence of the throng,
A democratic form of right divine
To rule first answerable to high design.
There is a call to life a little sterner,
And braver for the earner, learner, yearner.
Less criticism of the field and court
And more preoccupation with the sport.
It makes the prophet in us all presage
The glory of a next Augustan age
Of a power leading from its strength and pride,
Of young ambition eager to be tried,
Firm in our free beliefs without dismay,
In any game the nations want to play.
A golden age of poetry and power
Of which this noonday's the beginning hour.

THE GIFT OUTRIGHT

Robert Frost

The land was ours before we were the land's.
She was our land more than a hundred years
Before we were her people. She was ours
In Massachusetts, in Virginia,
But we were England's, still colonials,
Possessing what we still were unpossessed by,
Possessed by what we now no more possessed.
Something we were withholding made us weak
Until we found out that it was ourselves
We were withholding from our land of living,
And forthwith found salvation in surrender.
Such as we were we gave ourselves outright
(The deed of gift was many deeds of war)
To the land vaguely realizing westward,
But still unstoried, artless, unenhanced,
Such as she was, such as she would* become.

Spoken by the Author at the Inauguration of John F. Kennedy

At my father's request, Robert Frost substituted "would" to "will" when he spoke at the inauguration. Frost did not recite his poetry. Believing that poetry should capture the speech of the common man, he told people that he "said" his poems.

PAUL REVERE'S RIDE

Henry Wadsworth Longfellow

Listen, my children, and you shall hear
Of the midnight ride of Paul Revere
On the eighteenth of April, in Seventy-five;
Hardly a man is now alive
Who remembers that famous day and year.

He said to his friend, "If the British march
By land or sea from the town to-night,
Hang a lantern aloft in the belfry arch
Of the North Church tower as a signal light,—
One, if by land, and two, if by sea;
And I on the opposite shore will be,
Ready to ride and spread the alarm
Through every Middlesex village and farm,
For the country folk to be up and to arm."

Then he said "Good-night," and with muffled oar
Silently row'd to the Charlestown shore,
Just as the moon rose over the bay,
Where swinging wide at her moorings lay
The Somerset, British man-of-war;
A phantom ship, with each mast and spar
Across the moon like a prison bar,
And a huge black hulk, that was magnified
By its own reflection in the tide.

Meanwhile his friend, through alley and street,
Wanders and watches with eager ears,
Till in the silence around him he hears

The muster of men at the barrack-door,
The sound of arms, and the tramp of feet,
And the measured tread of the grenadiers
Marching down to their boats on the shore.

Then he climb'd the tower of the Old North Church,
By the wooden stairs, with stealthy tread,
To the belfry-chamber overhead,
And started the pigeons from their perch
On the sombre rafters, that round him made
Masses of moving shapes of shade,—
By the trembling ladder, steep and tall,
To the highest window in the wall,
Where he paused to listen and look down
A moment on the roofs of the town,
And the moonlight flowing over all.

Beneath, in the churchyard, lay the dead,
In their night-encampment on the hill,
Wrapp'd in silence so deep and still
That he could hear, like a sentinel's tread,
The watchful night-wind, as it went
Creeping along from tent to tent,
And seeming to whisper, "All is well!"
A moment only he feels the spell
Of the place and the hour, and the secret dread
Of the lonely belfry and the dead;
For suddenly all his thoughts are bent
On a shadowy something far away,
Where the river widens to meet the bay,—
A line of black that bends and floats
On the rising tide like a bridge of boats.

Meanwhile, impatient to mount and ride,
Booted and spurr'd, with a heavy stride
On the opposite shore walk'd Paul Revere.
Now he patted his horse's side,
Now gazed at the landscape far and near,
Then, impetuous, stamp'd the earth,
And turn'd and tighten'd his saddle-girth;
But mostly he watch'd with eager search
The belfry-tower of the Old North Church,
As it rose above the graves on the hill,
Lonely and spectral and sombre and still.
And lo! as he looks, on the belfry's height
A glimmer, and then a gleam of light!
He springs to the saddle, the bridle he turns,
But lingers and gazes, till full on his sight
A second lamp in the belfry burns.

A hurry of hoofs in a village street,
A shape in the moonlight, a bulk in the dark,
And beneath, from the pebbles, in passing, a spark
Struck out by a steed flying fearless and fleet:
That was all; and yet, through the gloom and the light,
The fate of a nation was riding that night;
And the spark struck out by that steed in his flight
Kindled the land into flame with its heat.

He has left the village and mounted the steep,
And beneath him, tranquil and broad and deep,
Is the Mystic, meeting the ocean tides,
And under the alders that skirt its edge,
Now soft on the sand, now loud on the ledge,
Is heard the tramp of his steed as he rides.

It was twelve by the village clock
When he cross'd the bridge into Medford town.
He heard the crowing of the cock,
And the barking of the farmer's dog,
And felt the damp of the river fog,
That rises after the sun goes down.

It was one by the village clock
When he galloped into Lexington.
He saw the gilded weathercock
Swim in the moonlight as he pass'd,
And the meeting-house windows, blank and bare,
Gaze at him with a spectral glare,
As if they already stood aghast
At the bloody work they would look upon.

It was two by the village clock
When he came to the bridge in Concord town.
He heard the bleating of the flock,
And the twitter of birds among the trees,
And felt the breath of the morning breeze
Blowing over the meadows brown.
And one was safe and asleep in his bed
Who at the bridge would be first to fall,
Who that day would be lying dead,
Pierced by a British musket-ball.

You know the rest; in the books you have read,
How the British regulars fired and fled,—
How the farmers gave them ball for ball,
From behind each fence and farmyard wall,
Chasing the red-coats down the lane,

Then crossing the fields to emerge again
Under the trees at the turn of the road,
And only pausing to fire and load.
So through the night rode Paul Revere,
And so through the night went his cry of alarm
To every Middlesex village and farm,—
A cry of defiance, and not of fear,
A voice in the darkness, a knock at the door,
And a word that shall echo for evermore!
For, borne on the night-wind of the Past,
Through all our history, to the last,
In the hour of darkness, and peril, and need,
The people will waken and listen to hear
The hurrying hoof-beats of that steed,
And the midnight message of Paul Revere.

I HEAR AMERICA SINGING

Walt Whitman

I hear America singing, the varied carols I hear,
Those of mechanics, each one singing his as it should be blithe
    and strong,
The carpenter singing his as he measures his plank or beam,
The mason singing his as he makes ready for work, or leaves
    off work,
The boatman singing what belongs to him in his boat, the
    deckhand singing on the steamboat deck,
The shoemaker singing as he sits on his bench, the hatter
    singing as he stands,
The wood-cutter's song, the ploughboy's on his way in the
    morning, or at noon intermission or at sundown,
The delicious singing of the mother, or of the young wife at
    work, or of the girl sewing or washing,
Each singing what belongs to him or her and to none else,
The day what belongs to the day—at night the party of young
    fellows, robust, friendly,
Singing with open mouths their strong melodious songs.

LET AMERICA BE AMERICA AGAIN
Langston Hughes

Let America be America again.
Let it be the dream it used to be.
Let it be the pioneer on the plain
Seeking a home where he himself is free.

(America never was America to me.)

Let America be the dream the dreamers dreamed—
Let it be that great strong land of love
Where never kings connive nor tyrants scheme
That any man be crushed by one above.

(It never was America to me.)

O, let my land be a land where Liberty
Is crowned with no false patriotic wreath,
But opportunity is real, and life is free,
Equality is in the air we breathe.

(There's never been equality for me,
Nor freedom in this "homeland of the free.")

Say who are you that mumbles in the dark?
And who are you that draws your veil across the stars?

I am the poor white, fooled and pushed apart,
I am the Negro bearing slavery's scars.
I am the red man driven from the land,

I am the immigrant clutching the hope I seek—
And finding only the same old stupid plan
Of dog eat dog, of mighty crush the weak.

I am the young man, full of strength and hope,
Tangled in that ancient endless chain
Of profit, power, gain, of grab the land!
Of grab the gold! Of grab the ways of satisfying need!
Of work the men! Of take the pay!
Of owning everything for one's own greed!

I am the farmer, bondsman to the soil.
I am the worker sold to the machine.
I am the Negro, servant to you all.
I am the people, worried, hungry, mean—
Hungry yet today despite the dream.
Beaten yet today—O, Pioneers!
I am the man who never got ahead,
The poorest worker bartered through the years.

Yet I'm the one who dreamt our basic dream
In that Old World while still a serf of kings,
Who dreamt a dream so strong, so brave, so true,
That even yet its mighty daring sings
In every brick and stone, in every furrow turned
That's made America the land it has become.
O, I'm the man who sailed those early seas
In search of what I meant to be my home—
For I'm the one who left dark Ireland's shore,
And Poland's plain, and England's grassy lea,
And torn from Black Africa's strand I came

To build a "homeland of the free."
The free?
A dream—
Still beckoning to me!

O, let America be America again—
The land that never has been yet—
And yet must be—
The land where *every* man is free.
The land that's mine—
The poor man's, Indian's, Negro's, ME—
Who made America,
Whose sweat and blood, whose faith and pain,
Whose hand at the foundry, whose plow in the rain,
Must bring back our mighty dream again.

Sure, call me any ugly name you choose—
The steel of freedom does not stain.
From those who live like leeches on the people's
    lives,
We must take back our land again,
America!

O, yes,
I say it plain,
America never was America to me,
And yet I swear this oath—
America will be!
An ever-living seed,
Its dream
Lies deep in the heart of me.

We, the people, must redeem
Our land, the mines, the plants, the rivers,
The mountains and the endless plain—
All, all the stretch of these great green states—
And make America again!

BROWN RIVER, SMILE

Jean Toomer

It is a new America,
To be spiritualized by each new American.

Lift, lift, thou waking forces!
Let us feel the energy of animals,
The energy of rumps and bull-bent heads
Crashing the barrier to man.
It must spiral on!
A million million men, or twelve men,
Must crash the barrier to the next higher form.

    Beyond plants are animals,
    Beyond animals is man,
    Beyond man is the universe.

    The Big Light,
    Let the Big Light in!

O thou, Radiant Incorporeal,
The I of earth and of mankind, hurl
Down these seaboards, across this continent,
The thousand-rayed discus of thy mind,
And above our walking limbs unfurl
Spirit-torsos of exquisite strength!

The Mississippi, sister of the Ganges,
Main artery of earth in the western world,
Is waiting to become

In the spirit of America, a sacred river.
Whoever lifts the Mississippi
Lifts himself and all America;
Whoever lifts himself
Makes that great brown river smile.
The blood of earth and the blood of man
Course swifter and rejoice when we spiritualize.
The old gods, led by an inverted Christ,
A shaved Moses, a blanched Lemur,
And a moulting thunderbird,
Withdrew into the distance and soon died,
Their dust and seed falling down
To fertilize the five regions of America.

We are waiting for a new God.

The old peoples—
The great European races sent wave after wave
That washed the forests, the earth's rich loam,
Grew towns with the seeds of giant cities,
Made roads, laid golden rails,
Sang once of its swift achievement,
And died congested in machinery.
They say that near the end
It was a world of crying men and hard women,
A city of goddam and Jehovah
Baptized in industry
Without benefit of saints,
Of dear defectives
Winnowing their likenesses from weathered rock
Sold by national organizations of undertakers.

Someone said:
    Suffering is impossible
    On cement sidewalks, in skyscrapers,
    In motorcars;
    Steel cannot suffer—
    We die unconsciously
    Because possessed by a nonhuman symbol.

Another cried:
    It is because of thee, O Life,
    That the first prayer ends in the last curse.

Another sang:
    Late minstrels of the restless earth,
    No muteness can be granted thee,
    Lift thy laughing energies
    To that white point which is a star.

The great African races sent a single wave
And singing riplets to sorrow in red fields,
Sing a swan song, to break rocks
And immortalize a hiding water boy.

    I'm leaving the shining ground, brothers,
    I sing because I ache,
    I go because I must,
    Brothers, I am leaving the shining ground;
    Don't ask me where,
    I'll meet you there,
    I'm leaving the shining ground.

The great red race was here.
In a land of flaming earth and torrent-rains,

Of red sea-plains and majestic mesas,
At sunset from a purple hill
The Gods came down;
They serpentined into pueblo,
And a white-robed priest
Danced with them five days and nights;
But pueblo, priest, and Shalicos
Sank into the sacred earth
To fertilize the five regions of America.

Hi-ye, hi-yo, hi-yo
Hi-ye, hi-yo, hi-yo,
A lone eagle feather,
An untamed Navaho,
The ghosts of buffaloes,
Hi-ye, hi-yo, hi-yo,
Hi-ye, hi-yo, hi-yo.

We are waiting for a new people.

O thou, Radiant Incorporeal,
The I of earth and of mankind, hurl
Down these seaboards, across this continent,
The thousand-rayed discus of thy mind,
And above our walking limbs unfurl
Spirit-torsos of exquisite strength!

The east coast is masculine,
The west coast is feminine,
The middle region is the child—
Forces of reconciling
And generator of symbols.

Thou, great fields, waving thy growths across the world,
Couldest thou find the seed which started thee?
Can you remember the first great hand to sow?
Have you memory of His intention?
Great plains, and thou, mountains,
And thou, stately trees, and thou,
America, sleeping and producing with the seasons,
No clever dealer can divide,
No machine can undermine thee.

The prairie's sweep is flat infinity,
The city's rise is perpendicular to farthest star,
I stand where the two directions intersect,
At Michigan Avenue and Walton Place,
Parallel to my countrymen,
Right-angled to the universe.

It is a new America,
To be spiritualized by each new American.

FIRST POEMS

WHEN I WAS JUST ABOUT THREE my mother taught me to recite "First Fig" and "Second Fig" by Edna St. Vincent Millay as a surprise for my father. I remember his delight, and my own. And for each holiday or birthday, John and I would have to write or choose a poem for my mother. We had to copy it down and illustrate it, and she pasted them all in a special scrapbook. A few days before Valentine's Day or Mother's Day, there would be a mad scramble for the poetry books, and a mild sense of competition to see whose poem was longer, or more famous. It wasn't like a school assignment, but an infinite wandering that took us out of our own world, and into so many others. Now my own children are carrying on that tradition, reading, choosing and writing poems for me and my husband. Almost all of the poems that follow are from the scrapbook, which has remained one of our most precious family possessions, and when I look at it now, I can see as much about each of us by reading the poems we chose as I can by looking at photographs.

Many of these poems come to life when they are read aloud. Some benefit from marching around the room, or stomping your feet, so I hope this section will be accompanied by a good deal of noise. Children are also deeply reflective, and respond to language expressing our most powerful emotions: faith, hope and the search for God.

My mother believed that children should be encouraged to read the great writers and poets. This section is just a starting point. Each of the other sections also contains poems for readers of all ages. I have tried to put the simpler poems first in the hope that they will lead readers of all ages to discover poems of many voices.

FIRST FIG
Edna St. Vincent Millay

My candle burns at both ends;
    It will not last the night;
But ah, my foes, and oh, my friends—
    It gives a lovely light!

SECOND FIG
Edna St. Vincent Millay

Safe upon the solid rock the ugly houses stand:
Come and see my shining palace built upon the sand!

FOG

Carl Sandburg

The fog comes
on little cat feet.
It sits looking
over harbor and city
on silent haunches
and then moves on.

Basho

An old silent pond . . .
A frog jumps into the pond,
Splash! Silence again.

Basho

Farewell! Like a bee
reluctant to leave the deeps
of a peony.

THE LAND OF COUNTERPANE

Robert Louis Stevenson

When I was sick and lay a-bed,
I had two pillows at my head,
And all my toys beside me lay
To keep me happy all the day.

And sometimes for an hour or so
I watched my leaden soldiers go,
With different uniforms and drills,
Among the bed-clothes, through the hills.

And sometimes sent my ships in fleets
All up and down among the sheets;
Or brought my trees and houses out,
And planted cities all about.

I was the giant great and still
That sits upon the pillow-hill,
And sees before him, dale and plain,
The pleasant land of Counterpane.

THE SWING

Robert Louis Stevenson

How do you like to go up in a swing,
    Up in the air so blue?
"Oh, I do think it the pleasantest thing
    Ever a child can do!"

"Up in the air and over the wall,
    Till I can see so wide,
Rivers and trees and cattle and all
    Over the countryside—

"Till I look down on the garden green
    Down on the roof so brown—
Up in the air I go flying again,
    Up in the air and down!"

BED IN SUMMER

Robert Louis Stevenson

In winter I get up at night
And dress by yellow candle-light.
In summer, quite the other way,
I have to go to bed by day.

I have to go to bed and see
The birds still hopping on the tree,
Or hear the grown-up people's feet
Still going past me in the street.

And does it not seem hard to you,
When all the sky is clear and blue,
And I should like so much to play,
To have to go to bed by day?

TEDDY BEAR'S PICNIC
Jimmy Kennedy

If you go down to the woods today
You're sure of a big surprise
If you go down to the woods today
You'd better go in disguise

For ev'ry bear that ever there was
Will gather there for certain, because
Today's the day the Teddy Bears have their picnic.

Ev'ry Teddy Bear who's been good
Is sure of a treat today.
There's lots of marvelous things to eat
And wonderful games to play

Beneath the trees where nobody sees
They'll hide and seek as long as they please
'Cause that's the way the Teddy Bears have their picnic

If you go down to the woods today
You'd better not go alone
It's lovely down in the woods today
But safer to stay at home

For ev'ry bear that ever there was
Will gather there for certain, because
Today's the day the Teddy Bears have their picnic.

Picnic time for Teddy Bears
The little Teddy Bears are having a lovely time today

Watch them, catch them unawares
And see them picnic on their holiday.

See them gaily gad about
They love to play and shout;
They never have any care;

At six o'clock their Mummies and Daddies,
Will take them home to bed,
Because they're tired little Teddy Bears.

THREE PONIES
Arthur Guiterman

Three little ponies who didn't like their hay
Said to each other "Let's run away!"
Said the first "I will canter!"
Said the second "I will trot!"
Said the third "I will run if it's not too hot!"

And they all started off
With their tails in the air.
But they couldn't jump the fence
So they're all still there.

THE YAK
Theodore Roethke

There was a most odious yak
Who took only toads on his back
If you asked for a ride
He would act very snide
And go humping off yickety yak

GRIZZLY BEAR

Mary Austin

If you ever ever meet a grizzly bear
You must never never never ask him where he is going,
Or what he is doing,
For if you ever ever dare,
To stop a grizzly bear,
You will never meet another grizzly bear.

THE ELEPHANT
Hilaire Belloc

When people call this beast to mind,
   They marvel more and more
At such a *little* tail behind
   So LARGE a trunk before.

THE LITTLE TURTLE
Vachel Lindsay

There was a little turtle.
He lived in a box.
He swam in a puddle.
He climbed on the rocks.

He snapped at a mosquito.
He snapped at a flea.
He snapped at a minnow.
And he snapped at me.

He caught the mosquito.
He caught the flea.
He caught the minnow.
But he didn't catch me.

DOGS AND WEATHER
Winifred Welles

I'd like a different dog
   For every kind of weather—
A narrow greyhound for a fog,
     A wolfhound strange and white,
    With a tail like a silver feather
     To run with in the night,
      When snow is still, and winter stars are bright.

In the fall I'd like to see
   In answer to my whistle,
A golden spaniel look at me.
    But best of all for rain
A terrier, hairy as a thistle,
     To trot with fine disdain
      Beside me down the soaked, sweet-smelling lane.

LITTLE TROTTY WAGTAIL

John Clare

Little trotty wagtail, he went in the rain,
And twittering, tottering sideways he ne'er got straight again.
He stooped to get a worm, and looked up to get a fly,
And then he flew away ere his feathers they were dry.

Little trotty wagtail, he waddled in the mud,
And left his little footmarks, trample where he would.
He waddled in the water-pudge, and waggle went his tail,
And chirrupt up his wings to dry upon the garden rail.

Little trotty wagtail, you nimble all about,
And in the dimpling water-pudge you waddle in and out;
Your home is nigh at hand, and in the warm pig-stye,
So, little Master Wagtail, I'll bid you a good-by.

THE OWL AND THE PUSSY-CAT

Edward Lear

The Owl and the Pussy-Cat went to sea
    In a beautiful pea-green boat:
They took some honey, and plenty of money
    Wrapped up in a five-pound note.
The Owl looked up to the stars above,
    And sang to a small guitar,
"O lovely Pussy, O Pussy, my love,
    What a beautiful Pussy you are,
        You are,
        You are!
    What a beautiful Pussy you are!"

Pussy said to the Owl, "You elegant fowl,
    How charmingly sweet you sing!
Oh! let us be married; too long we have tarried:
    But what shall we do for a ring?"
They sailed away, for a year and a day,
    To the land where the bong-tree grows;
And there in a wood a Piggy-wig stood,
    With a ring at the end of his nose,
        His nose,
        His nose,
    With a ring at the end of his nose.

"Dear Pig, are you willing to sell for one shilling
    Your ring?" Said the Piggy, "I will."
So they took it away, and were married next day
    By the turkey who lives on the hill.
They dined on mince and slices of quince,

Which they ate with a runcible spoon;
And hand in hand, on the edge of the sand,
They danced by the light of the moon,
The moon,
The moon,
They danced by the light of the moon.

THE CROCODILE
Lewis Carroll

How doth the little crocodile
 Improve his shining tail,
And pour the waters of the Nile
 On every golden scale!

How cheerfully he seems to grin,
 How neatly spreads his claws,
And welcomes little fishes in,
 With gently smiling jaws!

FIREFLIES IN THE GARDEN
Robert Frost

Here come real stars to fill the upper skies,
And here on earth come emulating flies,
That though they never equal stars in size,
(And they were never really stars at heart)
Achieve at times a very star-like start.
Only, of course, they can't sustain the part.

THE ROSE FAMILY

Robert Frost

The rose is a rose,
And was always a rose.
But the theory now goes
That the apple's a rose,
And the pear is, and so's
The plum, I suppose.
The dear only knows
What will next prove a rose.
You, of course, are a rose—
But were always a rose.

WHO HAS SEEN THE WIND?
Christina Rossetti

Who has seen the wind?
   Neither I nor you:
But when the leaves hang trembling,
   The wind is passing through.

Who has seen the wind?
   Neither you nor I:
But when the trees bow down their heads,
   The wind is passing by.

TARANTELLA

Hilaire Belloc

Do you remember an Inn,
Miranda?
Do you remember an Inn?
And the tedding and the spreading
Of the straw for a bedding,
And the fleas that tease in the High Pyrenees,
And the wine that tasted of the tar?
And the cheers and the jeers of the young muleteers
(Under the vine of the dark verandah)?
Do you remember an Inn, Miranda,
Do you remember an Inn?
And the cheers and the jeers of the young muleteers
Who hadn't got a penny,
And who weren't paying any,
And the hammer at the doors and the din?
And the *hip! hop! hap!*
Of the clap
Of the hands to the twirl and the swirl
Of the girl gone chancing,
Glancing,
Dancing,
Backing and advancing,
Snapping of the clapper to the spin
Out and in—
And the *ting, tong, tang* of the guitar!
Do you remember an Inn,
Miranda?
Do you remember an Inn?

Never more;
Miranda,
Never more.
Only the high peaks hoar:
And Aragon a torrent at the door.
No sound
In the walls of the halls where falls
The tread
Of the feet of the dead to the ground,
No sound:
But the boom
Of the far waterfall like doom.

SHERWOOD

Alfred Noyes

Sherwood in the twilight, is Robin Hood awake?
Gray and ghostly shadows are gliding through the brake;
Shadows of the dappled deer, dreaming of the morn,
Dreaming of a shadowy man that winds a shadowy horn.

Robin Hood is here again: all his merry thieves
Hear a ghostly bugle-note shivering through the leaves,
Calling as he used to call, faint and far away,
In Sherwood, in Sherwood, about the break of day.

Merry, merry England has kissed the lips of June;
All the wings of fairyland were here beneath the moon;
Like a flight of rose-leaves fluttering in a mist
Of opal and ruby and pearl and amethyst.

Merry, merry England is waking as of old,
With eyes of blither hazel and hair of brighter gold:
For Robin Hood is here again beneath the bursting spray
In Sherwood, in Sherwood, about the break of day.

Love is in the greenwood building him a house
Of wild rose and hawthorn and honeysuckle boughs;
Love is in the greenwood: dawn is in the skies;
And Marian is waiting with a glory in her eyes.

Hark! The dazzled laverock climbs the golden steep:
Marian is waiting: is Robin Hood asleep?

Round the fairy grass-rings frolic elf and fay,
In Sherwood, in Sherwood, about the break of day.

Oberon, Oberon, rake away the gold,
Rake away the red leaves, roll away the mold,
Rake away the gold leaves, roll away the red,
And wake Will Scarlet from his leafy forest bed.

Friar Tuck and Little John are riding down together
With quarter-staff and drinking-can and gray goose-feather;
The dead are coming back again; the years are rolled away
In Sherwood, in Sherwood, about the break of day.

Softly over Sherwood the south wind blows;
All the heart of England hid in every rose
Hears across the greenwood the sunny whisper leap,
Sherwood in the red dawn, is Robin Hood asleep?

Hark, the voice of England wakes him as of old
And, shattering the silence with a cry of brighter gold,
Bugles in the greenwood echo from the steep,
Sherwood in the red dawn, is Robin Hood asleep?

Where the deer are gliding down the shadowy glen
All across the glades of fern he calls his merry men;
Doublets of the Lincoln green glancing through the May,
In Sherwood, in Sherwood, about the break of day;

Calls them and they answer: from aisles of oak and ash
Rings the *Follow! Follow!* and the boughs begin to crash;

The ferns begin to flutter and the flowers begin to fly;
And through the crimson dawning the robber band goes by.

Robin! Robin! Robin! All his merry thieves
Answer as the bugle-note shivers through the leaves:
Calling as he used to call, faint and far away,
In Sherwood, in Sherwood, about the break of day.

ANNABEL LEE
Edgar Allan Poe

It was many and many a year ago,
    In a kingdom by the sea,
That a maiden there lived whom you may know
    By the name of Annabel Lee;—
And this maiden she lived with no other thought
    Than to love and be loved by me.

I was a child and *she* was a child,
    In this kingdom by the sea;
But we loved with a love that was more than love—
    I and my Annabel Lee—
With a love that the winged seraphs in Heaven
    Coveted her and me.

And this was the reason that, long ago,
    In this kingdom by the sea,
A wind blew out of a cloud, chilling
    My beautiful Annabel Lee;
So that her high-born kinsmen came
    And bore her away from me,
To shut her up in a sepulchre,
    In this kingdom by the sea.

The angels, not half so happy in Heaven,
    Went envying her and me—
Yes!—that was the reason (as all men know,
    In this kingdom by the sea)
That the wind came out of the cloud by night,
    Chilling and killing my Annabel Lee.

But our love it was stronger by far than the love
   Of those who were older than we—
   Of many far wiser than we—
And neither the angels in Heaven above,
   Nor the demons down under the sea,
Can ever dissever my soul from the soul
   Of the beautiful Annabel Lee:—

For the moon never beams, without bringing me dreams
   Of the beautiful Annabel Lee;
And the stars never rise, but I feel the bright eyes
   Of the beautiful Annabel Lee:—
And so, all the night-tide, I lie down by the side
Of my darling—my darling—my life and my bride,
   In her sepulchre there by the sea—
   In her tomb by the sounding sea.

SOME KEEP THE SABBATH GOING TO CHURCH

Emily Dickinson

Some keep the Sabbath going to church;
I keep it staying at home,
With a bobolink for a chorister,
And an orchard for a dome.

Some keep the Sabbath in surplice;
I just wear my wings,
And instead of tolling the bell for church
Our little sexton sings.

God preaches,—a noted clergyman,—
And the sermon is never long;
So instead of getting to heaven at last,
I'm going all along!

HOPE IS THE THING WITH FEATHERS
Emily Dickinson

Hope is the thing with feathers
That perches in the soul,
And sings the tune without the words,
And never stops at all,

And sweetest in the gale is heard;
And sore must be the storm
That could abash the little bird
That kept so many warm.

I've heard it in the chillest land,
And on the strangest sea;
Yet, never, in extremity,
It asked a crumb of me.

MOTHER TO SON

Langston Hughes

Well, son, I'll tell you:
Life for me ain't been no crystal stair.
It's had tacks in it,
And splinters,
And boards torn up,
And places with no carpet on the floor—
Bare.
But all the time
I'se been a-climbin' on,
And reachin' landin's,
And turnin' corners,
And sometimes goin' in the dark
Where there ain't been no light.
So, boy, don't you turn back.
Don't you set down on the steps
'Cause you finds it's kinder hard.
Don't you fall now—
For I'se still goin', honey,
I'se still climbin',
And life for me ain't been no crystal stair.

THE RED WHEELBARROW
William Carlos Williams

so much depends
upon

a red wheel
barrow

glazed with rain
water

beside the white
chickens.

My son Jack chose this poem.

A Psalm of David. The LORD is my shepherd; I shall not want.

He maketh me to lie down in green pastures: he leadeth me beside the still waters.

He restoreth my soul: he leadeth me in the paths of righteousness for his name's sake.

Yea, though I walk through the valley of the shadow of death, I will fear no evil: for thou art with me; thy rod and thy staff they comfort me.

Thou preparest a table before me in the presence of mine enemies: thou anointest my head with oil; my cup runneth over.

Surely goodness and mercy shall follow me all the days of my life: and I will dwell in the house of the LORD for ever.

My mother loved the King James version of the Bible, and had learned many verses by heart at school. She encouraged John to memorize this psalm when he was about seven, and he recited it at many family occasions.

And it came to pass in those days, that there went out a decree from Cæsar Augustus, that all the world should be taxed.

(*And* this taxing was first made when Cyrenius was governor of Syria.)

And all went to be taxed, every one into his own city.

And Joseph also went up from Galilee, out of the city of Nazareth, into Judæa, unto the city of David, which is called Bethlehem; (because he was of the house and lineage of David:)

To be taxed with Mary his espoused wife, being great with child.

And so it was, that, while they were there, the days were accomplished that she should be delivered.

And she brought forth her firstborn son, and wrapped him in swaddling clothes, and laid him in a manger; because there was no room for them in the inn.

And there were in the same country shepherds abiding in the field, keeping watch over their flock by night.

And, lo, the angel of the Lord came upon them, and the glory of the Lord shone round about them: and they were sore afraid.

And the angel said unto them, Fear not: for, behold, I bring you good tidings of great joy, which shall be to all people.

For unto you is born this day in the city of David a Saviour, which is Christ the Lord.

And this *shall* be a sign unto you; Ye shall find the babe wrapped in swaddling clothes, lying in a manger.

And suddenly there was with the angel a multitude of the heavenly host praising God, and saying,

Glory to God in the highest, and on earth peace, good will toward men.

A VISIT FROM ST. NICHOLAS

Clement Clarke Moore

'Twas the night before Christmas, when all through the house
Not a creature was stirring, not even a mouse;
The stockings were hung by the chimney with care,
In hopes that St. Nicholas soon would be there;
The children were nestled all snug in their beds,
While visions of sugar-plums danced in their heads;
And mamma in her kerchief, and I in my cap,
Had just settled our brains for a long winter's nap,—
When out on the lawn there arose such a clatter,
I sprang from my bed to see what was the matter.
Away to the window I flew like a flash,
Tore open the shutters and threw up the sash.
The moon on the breast of the new-fallen snow
Gave a lustre of midday to objects below;
When what to my wondering eyes should appear,
But a miniature sleigh and eight tiny reindeer,
With a little old driver, so lively and quick
I knew in a moment it must be St. Nick.
More rapid than eagles his coursers they came,
And he whistled and shouted, and called them by name:
"Now, Dasher! now, Dancer! now, Prancer and Vixen!
On, Comet! on, Cupid! on, Donder and Blitzen!
To the top of the porch, to the top of the wall!
Now dash away, dash away, dash away all!"
As dry leaves that before the wild hurricane fly,
When they meet with an obstacle, mount to the sky,
So up to the house-top the coursers they flew,
With the sleigh full of toys,—and St. Nicholas too.
And then in a twinkling I heard on the roof

The prancing and pawing of each little hoof.
As I drew in my head, and was turning around,
Down the chimney St. Nicholas came with a bound.
He was dressed all in fur from his head to his foot,
And his clothes were all tarnished with ashes and soot;
A bundle of toys he had flung on his back,
And he looked like a pedlar just opening his pack.
His eyes, how they twinkled! his dimples, how merry!
His cheeks were like roses, his nose like a cherry;
His droll little mouth was drawn up like a bow,
And the beard on his chin was as white as the snow.
The stump of a pipe he held tight in his teeth,
And the smoke it encircled his head like a wreath.
He had a broad face and a little round belly
That shook, when he laughed, like a bowl full of jelly.
He was chubby and plump,—a right jolly old elf;
And I laughed, when I saw him, in spite of myself.
A wink of his eye and a twist of his head
Soon gave me to know I had nothing to dread.
He spoke not a word, but went straight to his work,
And filled all the stockings; then turned with a jerk,
And laying his finger aside of his nose,
And giving a nod, up the chimney he rose.
He sprang to his sleigh, to his team gave a whistle,
And away they all flew like the down of a thistle;
But I heard him exclaim, ere he drove out of sight,
"Happy Christmas to all, and to all a good-night!"

ADVENTURE

MY MOTHER LIVED HER LIFE with a spirit of adventure. She loved to ride horses at full gallop, explore faraway places, and read about those who approached life the same way. This same spirit of adventure, combined with her knowledge and love of history, allowed her to describe life under an Egyptian pharaoh, the heroism of the ancient Athenians, or the courtly intrigues of eighteenth-century France so vividly that John and I could imagine ourselves transported in time.

Her childhood heroes were Mowgli and Robin Hood, and they became ours as well. Later, when we spent time in Greece, we came to share her love of the *Odyssey* and the adventures of Ulysses. She took us to the Strait of Messina so we could see how the poet had transformed the natural world into the image of Scylla and Charybdis, and we went to Ithaca.

She shared this love of heroic adventure with my father. One poem that was special to both of them was Alfred Lord Tennyson's "Ulysses." My mother had memorized it with her grandfather when she was ten years old. She introduced it to my father who often quoted from it in his speeches, and later the poem became identified with my uncle Bobby as well. Their favorite lines were:

Come my friends
'Tis not too late to seek a newer world . . .
Though much is taken, much abides;
   . . . that which we are we are,—
One equal temper of heroic hearts,
Made weak by time and fate, but strong in will
To strive, to seek, to find, and not to yield.

Both my parents loved reading Shakespeare. While my mother was drawn to the love poetry, my father preferred the history plays. One of his favorite passages was Henry V's St. Crispin's Day speech. It describes the honor of having risked one's life for one's country at a moment when it truly mattered. When my mother planned an evening of Elizabethan poetry and music at the White House, as a surprise for my father, she ended that evening's program with the speech from *Henry V*.

"Speed, bonnie boat, like a bird on the wing, Onward," the
    sailors cry!
"Carry the lad that's born to be king Over the sea to Skye."

Loud the winds howl, loud the waves roar, Thunder clouds
    rend the air;
Baffled our foes stand on the shore, Follow they will not
    dare.

"Speed, bonnie boat, like a bird on the wing, Onward," the
    sailors cry!
"Carry the lad that's born to be king Over the sea to Skye."

Though the waves leap, soft shall ye sleep, Ocean's a royal bed;
Rock'd in the deep, Flora will keep Watch by your weary
    head.

"Speed, bonnie boat, like a bird on the wing, Onward," the
    sailors cry!
"Carry the lad that's born to be king Over the sea to Skye."

Many's the lad fought on that day, Well the claymore could
    wield,
When the night came, silently lay, Dead on Culloden's field.

"Speed, bonnie boat, like a bird on the wing, Onward," the
    sailors cry!
Carry the lad that's born to be king Over the sea to Skye."

Burn'd are our homes, exile and death Scatter the loyal men;
Yet, ere the sword cool in the sheath, Charlie will come again.

"Speed, bonnie boat, like a bird on the wing, Onward," the
sailors cry!
"Carry the lad that's born to be king Over the sea to Skye."

CARGOES

John Masefield

Quinquireme of Nineveh from distant Ophir
Rowing home to haven in sunny Palestine,
With a cargo of ivory,
And apes and peacocks,
Sandalwood, cedarwood, and sweet white wine.

Stately Spanish galleon coming from the Isthmus,
Dipping through the Tropics by the palm-green shores,
With a cargo of diamonds,
Emeralds, amethysts,
Topazes, and cinnamon, and gold moidores.

Dirty British coaster with a salt-caked smoke stack
Butting through the Channel in the mad March days,
With a cargo of Tyne coal,
Road-rail, pig-lead,
Firewood, iron-ware, and cheap tin trays.

SEA-FEVER

John Masefield

I must go down to the seas again, to the lonely sea and the sky,
And all I ask is a tall ship and a star to steer her by,
And the wheel's kick and the wind's song and the white sail's
    shaking
And a gray mist on the sea's face and a gray dawn breaking.

I must go down to the seas again, for the call of the running
    tide
Is a wild call and a clear call that may not be denied;
And all I ask is a windy day with the white clouds flying,
And the flung spray and the blown spume, and the sea-gulls
    crying.

I must go down to the seas again, to the vagrant gypsy life,
To the gull's way and the whale's way where the wind's like a
    whetted knife;
And all I ask is a merry yarn from a laughing fellow-rover,
And quiet sleep and a sweet dream when the long trick's over.

HUNTING-SONG OF THE SEEONEE PACK
Rudyard Kipling

As the dawn was breaking the Sambhur belled
   Once, twice and again!
And a doe leaped up and a doe leaped up
From the pond in the wood where the wild deer sup.
This I, scouting alone, beheld,
   Once, twice and again!

As the dawn was breaking the Sambhur belled
   Once, twice and again!
And a wolf stole back and a wolf stole back
To carry the word to the waiting pack,
And we sought and we found and we bayed on his track
   Once, twice and again!

As the dawn was breaking the Wolf Pack yelled
   Once, twice and again!
Feet in the jungle that leave no mark!
Eyes that can see in the dark—the dark!
Tongue—give tongue to it! Hark! O hark!
   Once, twice and again!

This poem is from The Jungle Book, *which was my mother's favorite book when she was a child.*

TABLEAU
Countee Cullen

For Donald Duff

Locked arm in arm they cross the way,
   The black boy and the white,
The golden splendor of the day,
   The sable pride of night.

From lowered blinds the dark folk stare,
   And here the fair folk talk,
Indignant that these two should dare
   In unison to walk.

Oblivious to look and word
   They pass, and see no wonder
That lightning brilliant as a sword
   Should blaze the path of thunder.

MERRY-GO-ROUND

Langston Hughes

Where is the Jim Crow section
On this merry-go-round,
Mister, cause I want to ride?
Down South where I come from
White and colored
Can't sit side by side.
Down South on the train
There's a Jim Crow car.
On the bus we're put in the back—
But there ain't no back
To a merry-go-round!
Where's the horse
For a kid that's black?

THE ROAD NOT TAKEN

Robert Frost

Two roads diverged in a yellow wood,
And sorry I could not travel both
And be one traveler, long I stood
And looked down one as far as I could
To where it bent in the undergrowth;

Then took the other, as just as fair,
And having perhaps the better claim,
Because it was grassy and wanted wear;
Though as for that the passing there
Had worn them really about the same,

And both that morning equally lay
In leaves no step had trodden black.
Oh, I kept the first for another day!
Yet knowing how way leads on to way,
I doubted if I should ever come back.

I shall be telling this with a sigh
Somewhere ages and ages hence:
Two roads diverged in a wood, and I—
I took the one less traveled by,
And that has made all the difference.

SONG

John Donne

Go and catch a falling star,
    Get with child a mandrake root,
Tell me where all past years are,
    Or who cleft the Devil's foot;
Teach me to hear mermaids singing,
Or to keep off envy's stinging,
        And find
        What wind
Serves to advance an honest mind.

If thou be'st born to strange sights,
    Things invisible to see,
Ride ten thousand days and nights
    Till Age snow white hairs on thee;
Thou, when thou return'st, wilt tell me
All strange wonders that befell thee,
        And swear
        No where
Lives a woman true and fair.

If thou find'st one, let me know;
    Such a pilgrimage were sweet.
Yet do not; I would not go,
    Though at next door we might meet.
Though she were true when you met her,
And last till you write your letter,
        Yet she
        Will be
False, ere I come, to two or three.

My mother selected this poem along with "Death, be not proud" (p. 143) to show two different moods of the poet John Donne, to be read at the White House, April 30, 1963, Evening of Elizabethan Music and Poetry in Honor of the Grand Duchess and Prince of Luxembourg

William Shakespeare

Gloucester: Now is the winter of our discontent
Made glorious summer by this sun of York;
And all the clouds that lour'd upon our house
In the deep bosom of the ocean buried.
Now are our brows bound with victorious wreaths;
Our bruised arms hung up for monuments;
Our stern alarums changed to merry meetings;
Our dreadful marches to delightful measures.
Grim-visag'd war hath smooth'd his wrinkled front;
And now,—instead of mounting barbed steeds,
To fright the souls of fearful adversaries,—
He capers nimbly in a lady's chamber
To the lascivious pleasing of a lute.

William Shakespeare

King Henry: This day is call'd the feast of Crispian:
He that outlives this day, and comes safe home,
Will stand a tip-toe when this day is nam'd,
And rouse him at the name of Crispian.
He that shall live this day, and see old age,
Will yearly on the vigil feast his neighbours,
And say, 'To-morrow is Saint Crispian:'
Then will he strip his sleeve and show his scars,
And say, 'These wounds I had on Crispin's day.'
Old men forget: yet all shall be forgot,
But he'll remember with advantages
What feats he did that day. Then shall our names,
Familiar in his mouth as household words,
Harry the king, Bedford and Exeter,
Warwick and Talbot, Salisbury and Gloucester,
Be in their flowing cups freshly remember'd.
This story shall the good man teach his son;
And Crispin Crispian shall ne'er go by,
From this day to the ending of the world,
But we in it shall be remembered;
We few, we happy few, we band of brothers;
For he to-day that sheds his blood with me
Shall be my brother; be he ne'er so vile
This day shall gentle his condition:
And gentlemen in England now a-bed
Shall think themselves accurs'd they were not here,
And hold their manhoods cheap whiles any speaks
That fought with us upon Saint Crispin's day.

THE ISLES OF GREECE

George Gordon, Lord Byron

The isles of Greece! the isles of Greece
   Where burning Sappho loved and sung,
Where grew the arts of war and peace,
   Where Delos rose, and Phœbus sprung!
Eternal summer gilds them yet,
But all, except their sun, is set.

The Scian and the Teian muse,
   The hero's harp, the lover's lute,
Have found the fame your shores refuse:
   Their place of birth alone is mute
To sounds which echo further west
Than your sires' 'Islands of the Blest.

The mountains look on Marathon—
   And Marathon looks on the sea;
And musing there an hour alone,
   I dream'd that Greece might still be free;
For standing on the Persians' grave,
I could not deem myself a slave.

A king sate on the rocky brow
   Which looks o'er sea-born Salamis;
And ships, by thousands, lay below,
   And men in nations;—all were his!
He counted them at break of day—
And when the sun set, where were they?

And where are they? and where art thou,
　　My country? On thy voiceless shore
The heroic lay is tuneless now—
　　The heroic bosom beats no more!
And must thy lyre, so long divine,
Degenerate into hands like mine?

'Tis something in the dearth of fame,
　　Though link'd among a fetter'd race,
To feel at least a patriot's shame,
　　Even as I sing, suffuse my face;
For what is left the poet here?
For Greeks a blush—for Greece a tear.

Must *we* but weep o'er days more blest?
　　Must *we* but blush?—Our fathers bled.
Earth! render back from out thy breast
　　A remnant of our Spartan dead!
Of the three hundred grant but three,
To make a new Thermopylæ!

What, silent still? and silent all?
　　Ah! no;—the voices of the dead
Sound like a distant torrent's fall,
　　And answer, 'Let one living head,
But one, arise,—we come, we come!'
'Tis but the living who are dumb.

In vain—in vain: strike other chords;
　　Fill high the cup with Samian wine!
Leave battles to the Turkish hordes,

And shed the blood of Scio's vine!
Hark! rising to the ignoble call—
How answers each bold Bacchanal!

You have the Pyrrhic dance as yet;
      Where is the Pyrrhic phalanx gone?
Of two such lessons, why forget
      The nobler and the manlier one?
You have the letters Cadmus gave—
Think ye he meant them for a slave?

Fill high the bowl with Samian wine!
      We will not think of themes like these!
It made Anacreon's song divine:
      He served—but served Polycrates—
A tyrant; but our masters then
Were still, at least, our countrymen.

The tyrant of the Chersonese
      Was freedom's best and bravest friend;
That tyrant was Miltiades!
      O that the present hour would lend
Another despot of the kind!
Such chains as his were sure to bind.

Fill high the bowl with Samian wine!
      On Suli's rock, and Parga's shore,
Exists the remnant of a line
      Such as the Doric mothers bore;
And there, perhaps, some seed is sown,
The Heracleidan blood might own.

Trust not for freedom to the Franks—
    They have a king who buys and sells;
In native swords and native ranks
    The only hope of courage dwells:
But Turkish force and Latin fraud
Would break your shield, however broad.

Fill high the bowl with Samian wine!
    Our virgins dance beneath the shade—
I see their glorious black eyes shine;
    But gazing on each glowing maid,
My own the burning tear-drop laves,
To think such breasts must suckle slaves.

Place me on Sunium's marbled steep,
    Where nothing, save the waves and I,
May hear our mutual murmurs sweep;
    There, swan-like, let me sing and die:
A land of slaves shall ne'er be mine—
Dash down yon cup of Samian wine!

ULYSSES

Alfred Lord Tennyson

It little profits that an idle king,
By this still hearth, among these barren crags,
Matched with an aged wife, I mete and dole
Unequal laws unto a savage race,
That hoard, and sleep, and feed, and know not me.
I cannot rest from travel; I will drink
Life to the lees. All times I have enjoyed
Greatly, have suffered greatly, both with those
That loved me, and alone; on shore, and when
Through scudding drifts the rainy Hyades
Vext the dim sea. I am become a name;
For always roaming with a hungry heart
Much have I seen and known,—cities of men
And manners, climates, councils, governments,
Myself not least, but honoured of them all,—
And drunk delight of battle with my peers,
Far on the ringing plains of windy Troy.
I am a part of all that I have met;
Yet all experiences is an arch wherethrough
Gleams that untravelled world whose margin fades
For ever and for ever when I move.
How dull it is to pause, to make an end,
To rust unburnished, not to shine in use!
As though to breathe were life! Life piled on life
Were all too little, and of one to me
Little remains; but every hour is saved
From that eternal silence, something more,
A bringer of new things; and vile it were
For some three sums to store and hoard myself,

And this gray spirit yearning in desire
To follow knowledge like a sinking star,
Beyond the utmost bound of human thought.

This is my son, mine own Telemachus,
To whom I leave the sceptre and the isle,—
Well-loved of me, discerning to fulfill
This labour, by slow prudence to make mild
A rugged people, and through soft degrees
Subdue them to the useful and the good.
Most blameless is he, centred in the sphere
Of common duties, decent not to fail
In offices of tenderness, and pay
Meet adoration to my household gods,
When I am gone. He works his work, I mine.
There lies the port; the vessel puffs her sail;
There gloom the dark, broad seas. My mariners,
Souls that have toiled and wrought, and thought with me,—
That ever with a frolic welcome took
The thunder and the sunshine, and opposed
Free hearts, free foreheads,—you and I are old;
Old age hath yet his honour and his toil.
Death closes all; but something ere the end,
Some work of noble note, may yet be done,
Not unbecoming men that strove with Gods.
The lights begin to twinkle from the rocks;
The long day wanes; the slow moon climbs; the deep
Moans round with many voices. Come, my friends,
'Tis not too late to seek a newer world.
Push off, and sitting well in order smite
The sounding furrows; for my purpose holds
To sail beyond the sunset, and the baths

Of all the western stars, until I die.
It may be that the gulfs will wash us down;
It may be we shall touch the Happy Isles,
And see the great Achilles, whom we knew.
Though much is taken, much abides; and though
We are not now that strength which in old days
Moved earth and heaven, that which we are, we are,—
One equal temper of heroic hearts,
Made weak by time and fate, but strong in will
To strive, to seek, to find, and not to yield.

ITHACA
Constantine P. Cavafy

When you set out on your journey to Ithaca,
pray that the road is long,
full of adventure, full of knowledge.
The Lestrygonians and the Cyclops,
the angry Poseidon—do not fear them:
You will never find such as these on your path,
if your thoughts remain lofty, if a fine
emotion touches your spirit and your body.
The Lestrygonians and the Cyclops,
the fierce Poseidon you will never encounter,
if you do not carry them within your soul,
if your soul does not set them up before you.

Pray that the road is long.
That the summer mornings are many, when,
with such pleasure, with such joy
you will enter ports seen for the first time;
stop at Phoenician markets,
and purchase fine merchandise,
mother-of-pearl and coral, amber, and ebony,
and sensual perfumes of all kinds,
as many sensual perfumes as you can;
visit many Egyptian cities,
to learn and learn from scholars.

Always keep Ithaca in your mind.
To arrive there is your ultimate goal.
But do not hurry the voyage at all.
It is better to let it last for many years;

and to anchor at the island when you are old,
rich with all you have gained on the way,
not expecting that Ithaca will offer you riches.

Ithaca has given you the beautiful voyage.
Without her you would have never set out on the road.
She has nothing more to give you.

And if you find her poor, Ithaca has not deceived you.
Wise as you have become, with so much experience,
you must already have understood what these Ithacas mean.

ESCAPE

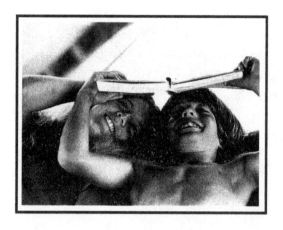

AS A CHILD, the poems I loved best were those like W. B. Yeats's "The Song of Wandering Aengus," where the distance isn't far between the world we live in and an entirely different and magical one. My mother sparked this interest by making these poems part of our daily lives, awakening in us a sense of limitless possibility. When we drove past the East River and saw the tugboats pushing their barges, we would talk about all the faraway places to go, and how other travelers had gotten there. She would quote lines from *The Odyssey* and "Sailing to Byzantium" by W. B. Yeats.

Not only was poetry part of our family life, it was also a source of fun. Because of her knowledge, my mother was in great demand for all sorts of games, but the best of all was to be on her charades team. She often preferred to read rather than play noisy games. But when we could convince her to play, she always came up with lines of poetry the other team had never even heard of (yet of course were too embarrassed to call unfair) and took great satisfaction in her triumph.

An exploration of the natural world can also be a form of escape, bringing refuge. Each season, too, inspires its own celebration— the stillness of winter, the excitement of spring, the delirium of summer, the nostalgia of autumn. My mother's birthday was in the summer, so the poems "Ariel's Song" and "I Taste a Liquor Never Brewed" always remind me of her.

THE FLOWERS

Robert Louis Stevenson

All the names I know from nurse:
Gardener's garters, Shepherd's purse,
Bachelor's buttons, Lady's smock,
And the Lady Hollyhock.

Fairy places, fairy things,
Fairy woods where the wild bee wings,
Tiny trees for tiny dames—
These must all be fairy names!

Tiny woods below whose boughs
Shady fairies weave a house;
Tiny tree-tops, rose or thyme,
Where the braver fairies climb!

Fair are grown-up people's trees,
But the fairest woods are these;
Where if I were not so tall,
I should live for good and all.

BEHIND STOWE

Elizabeth Bishop

I heard an elf go whistling by,
A whistle sleek as moonlit grass,
That drew me like a silver string
To where the dusty, pale moths fly,
And make a magic as they pass;
And there I heard a cricket sing.

His singing echoed through and through
The dark under a windy tree
Where glinted little insects' wings.
His singing split the sky in two.
The halves fell either side of me,
And I stood straight, bright with moon-rings.

IN JUST-SPRING

E. E. Cummings

in Just-
spring   when the world is mud-
luscious the little
lame balloonman

whistles   far   and wee

and eddieandbill come
running from marbles and
piracies and it's
spring

when the world is puddle-wonderful

the queer
old balloonman whistles
far   and   wee
and bettyandisbel come dancing

from hop-scotch and jump-rope and

it's
spring
and
        the

            goat-footed

balloonman   whistles

far
and
wee

THE PASTURE
Robert Frost

I'm going out to clean the pasture spring;
I'll only stop to rake the leaves away
(And wait to watch the water clear, I may):
I sha'n't be gone long.—You come too.

I'm going out to fetch the little calf
That's standing by the mother. It's so young,
It totters when she licks it with her tongue.
I sha'n't be gone long.—You come too.

PORTRAIT BY A NEIGHBOUR

Edna St. Vincent Millay

Before she has her floor swept
　　Or her dishes done,
Any day you'll find her
　　A-sunning in the sun!

It's long after midnight
　　Her key's in the lock,
And you never see her chimney smoke
　　Till past ten o'clock!

She digs in her garden
　　With a shovel and a spoon,
She weeds her lazy lettuce
　　By the light of the moon,

She walks up the walk
　　Like a woman in a dream,
She forgets she borrowed butter
　　And pays you back cream!

Her lawn looks like a meadow,
　　And if she mows the place
She leaves the clover standing
　　And the Queen Anne's lace!

THE SONG OF WANDERING AENGUS

William Butler Yeats

I went out to the hazel wood,
Because a fire was in my head,
And cut and peeled a hazel wand,
And hooked a berry to a thread;
And when white moths were on the wing,
And moth-like stars were flickering out,
I dropped the berry in a stream
And caught a little silver trout.

When I had laid it on the floor
I went to blow the fire aflame,
But something rustled on the floor,
And some one called me by my name:
It had become a glimmering girl
With apple blossom in her hair
Who called me by my name and ran
And faded through the brightening air.

Though I am old with wandering
Through hollow lands and hilly lands,
I will find out where she has gone,
And kiss her lips and take her hands;
And walk among long dappled grass,
And pluck till time and times are done
The silver apples of the moon,
The golden apples of the sun.

THE LAKE ISLE OF INNISFREE

William Butler Yeats

I will arise and go now, and go to Innisfree,
And a small cabin build there, of clay and wattles made:
Nine bean-rows will I have there, a hive for the honeybee,
And live alone in the bee-loud glade.

And I shall have some peace there, for peace comes dropping
     slow,
Dropping from the veils of the morning to where the cricket
     sings;
There midnight's all a glimmer, and noon a purple glow,
And evening full of the linnet's wings.

I will arise and go now, for always night and day
I hear lake water lapping with low sounds by the shore;
While I stand on the roadway, or on the pavements grey,
I hear it in the deep heart's core.

THE ODYSSEY

BOOK IX

Homer, translated by Robert Fitzgerald

Now all day long until the sun went down
we made our feast on mutton and sweet wine,
till after sunset in the gathering dark
we went to sleep above the wash of ripples.

When the young Dawn with finger tips of rose
touched the world, I roused the men, gave orders
to man the ships, cast off the mooring lines;
and filing in to sit beside the rowlocks
oarsmen in line dipped oars in the grey sea.
So we moved out, sad in the vast offing,
having our precious lives, but not our friends.

THE TEMPEST, V, i, 104–110
William Shakespeare

Ariel: Where the bee sucks, there suck I:
   In a cowslip's bell I lie;
There I couch when owls do cry.
On the bat's back I do fly
After summer merrily:
   Merrily, merrily, shall I live now,
   Under the blossom that hangs on the bough.

I TASTE A LIQUOR NEVER BREWED
Emily Dickinson

I taste a liquor never brewed,
    From tankards scooped in pearl;
Not Frankfort berries yield the sense
    Such a delirious whirl.

Inebriate of air am I,
    And debauchee of dew;—
Reeling through endless summer days,
    From inns of molten blue.

When landlords turn the drunken bee
    Out of the Fox-glove's door,
When butterflies renounce their drams,
    I shall but drink the more;

Till seraphs swing their snowy hats,
    And saint to windows run,
To see the little tippler
    Come staggering toward the sun.

THESE ARE THE DAYS WHEN BIRDS COME BACK
Emily Dickinson

These are the days when birds come back,
A very few, a bird or two,
To take a backward look.

These are the days when skies put on
The old, old sophistries of June,—
A blue and gold mistake.

Oh, fraud that cannot cheat the bee,
Almost thy plausibility
Induces my belief,

Till ranks of seeds their witness bear
And softly through the altered air
Hurries a timid leaf!

Oh, sacrament of summer days,
Oh, last communion in the haze,
Permit a child to join,

Thy sacred emblems to partake,
Thy consecrated bread to break,
Taste thine immortal wine!

STOPPING BY WOODS ON A SNOWY EVENING
Robert Frost

Whose woods these are I think I know.
His house is in the village though;
He will not see me stopping here
To watch his woods fill up with snow.

My little horse must think it queer
To stop without a farmhouse near
Between the woods and frozen lake
The darkest evening of the year.

He gives his harness bells a shake
To ask if there is some mistake.
The only other sound's the sweep
Of easy wind and downy flake.

The woods are lovely, dark and deep.
But I have promises to keep,
And miles to go before I sleep,
And miles to go before I sleep.

My father used to quote the last stanza of this poem in his speeches.

KUBLA KHAN
Samuel Taylor Coleridge

In Xanadau did Kubla Khan
   A stately pleasure-dome decree:
Where Alph, the sacred river, ran
Through caverns measureless to man
   Down to a sunless sea.
So twice five miles of fertile ground
With walls and towers were girdled round:
And there were gardens bright with sinuous rills,
Where blossomed many an incense-bearing tree;
And here were forests ancient as the hills,
Enfolding sunny spots of greenery.

But O! that deep romantic chasm which slanted
Down the green hill athwart a cedarn cover!
A savage place! as holy and enchanted
As e'er beneath a waning moon was haunted
By woman wailing for her demon-lover!
And from this chasm, with ceaseless turmoil seething,
As if this Earth in fast thick pants were breathing,
A mighty fountain momently was forced,
Amid whose swift half-intermitted burst
Huge fragments vaulted like rebounding hail,
Or chaffy grain beneath the thresher's flail:
And 'mid these dancing rocks at once and ever
It flung up momently the sacred river.
Five miles meandering with a mazy motion
Through wood and dale the sacred river ran,
Then reached the caverns measureless to man,
And sank in tumult to a lifeless ocean:

And 'mid this tumult Kubla heard from far
Ancestral voices prophesying war!

    The shadow of the dome of pleasure
    Floated midway on the waves;
    Where was heard the mingled measure
    From the fountain and the caves.
It was a miracle of rare device,
A sunny pleasure-dome with caves of ice!

    A damsel with a dulcimer
    In a vision once I saw:
    It was an Abyssinian maid,
    And on her dulcimer she played,
    Singing of Mount Abora.
    Could I revive within me
    Her symphony and song,
    To such a deep delight 'twould win me
That with music loud and long,
I would build that dome in air,
That sunny dome! those caves of ice!
And all who heard should see them there,
And all should cry, Beware! Beware!
His flashing eyes, his floating hair!
Weave a circle round him thrice,
And close your eyes with holy dread,
For he on honey-dew hath fed,
And drunk the milk of Paradise.

THE DAWN

William Butler Yeats

I would be ignorant as the dawn
That has looked down
On that old queen measuring a town
With the pin of a brooch,
Or on the withered men that saw
From their pedantic Babylon
The careless planets in their courses,
The stars fade out where the moon comes,
And took their tablets and did sums;
I would be ignorant as the dawn
That merely stood, rocking the glittering coach
Above the cloudy shoulders of the horses;
I would be—for no knowledge is worth a straw—
Ignorant and wanton as the dawn.

SAILING TO BYZANTIUM

William Butler Yeats

I

That is no country for old men. The young
In one another's arms, birds in the trees
—Those dying generations—at their song,
The salmon-falls, the mackerel-crowded seas,
Fish, flesh, or fowl, commend all summer long
Whatever is begotten, born, and dies.
Caught in that sensual music all neglect
Monuments of unageing intellect.

II

An aged man is but a paltry thing,
A tattered coat upon a stick, unless
Soul clap its hands and sing, and louder sing
For every tatter in its mortal dress,
Nor is there singing school but studying
Monuments of its own magnificence;
And therefore I have sailed the seas and come
To the holy city of Byzantium.

III

O sages standing in God's holy fire
As in the gold mosaic of a wall,
Come from the holy fire, perne in a gyre,
And be the singing-masters of my soul.
Consume my heart away; sick with desire
And fastened to a dying animal
It knows not what it is; and gather me
Into the artifice of eternity.

IV

Once out of nature I shall never take
My bodily form from any natural thing,
But such a form as Grecian goldsmiths make
Of hammered gold and gold enamelling
To keep a drowsy Emperor awake;
Or set upon a golden bough to sing
To lords and ladies of Byzantium
Of what is past, or passing, or to come.

OF MERE BEING

Wallace Stevens

The palm at the end of the mind,
Beyond the last thought, rises
In the bronze decor,

A gold-feathered bird
Sings in the palm, without human meaning,
Without human feeling, a foreign song.

You know then that it is not the reason
That makes us happy or unhappy.
The bird sings. Its feathers shine.

The palm stands on the edge of space.
The wind moves slowly in the branches.
The bird's fire-fangled feathers dangle down.

ROMANCE AND LOVE

MY MOTHER WAS A TRUE ROMANTIC. She lived her life on a dramatic scale and responded to the poetry of love with a passionate intensity. Lord Byron and Sir Walter Raleigh were two poets she admired. Both were men of action and of letters, both were adventurers and noblemen. Raleigh was a pirate, explorer, and natural scientist imprisoned by a jealous queen; Byron a freedom fighter and romantic hero.

One of my mother's favorite White House events was an evening of Elizabethan poetry and music featuring the actor Basil Rathbone. She worked hard on every detail of the evening, choosing the music to be played on Elizabethan instruments and overruling the Library of Congress and other Shakespearean scholars to make sure that her favorite poems were included in the program. "I have loaded it with love sonnets," she wrote in a triumphant memo discussing the pros and cons of various passages. I have included her favorites of the poems that were read that night—"Shall I Compare Thee to a Summer's Day," "The

Passionate Shepherd to His Love" (to which Raleigh wrote a reply), and others that she suggested, like "Is this the face that launched a thousand ships?"

Sometimes, poems like these can seem old-fashioned. The language is complex, the flowery style at odds with modern life and the changing roles of men and women. But if you do make the effort, you will find that the emotions these poets express are not foreign or faraway but ones that all of us have felt for those we love.

The voice of my beloved! behold, he cometh leaping upon the mountains, skipping upon the hills.

My beloved is like a roe or a young hart: behold, he standeth behind our wall, he looketh forth at the windows, shewing himself through the lattice.

My beloved spake, and said unto me, Rise up, my love, my fair one, and come away.

For, lo, the winter is past, the rain is over *and* gone;

The flowers appear on the earth; the time of the singing *of birds* is come, and the voice of the turtle is heard in our land;

The fig tree putteth forth her green figs, and the vines *with* the tender grape give a *good* smell. Arise, my love, my fair one, and come away.

O my dove, *that art* in the clefts of the rock, in the secret *places* of the stairs, let me see thy countenance, let me hear thy voice; for sweet *is* thy voice, and thy countenance *is* comely.

Take us the foxes, the little foxes, that spoil the vines: for our vines *have* tender grapes.

My beloved *is* mine, and I *am* his: he feedeth among the lilies.

PARADISE LOST

BOOK IV, 639–658

John Milton

With thee conversing, I forget all time,
All seasons, and their change; all please alike.
Sweet is the breath of Morn, her rising sweet,
With charm of earliest birds; pleasant the Sun,
When first on this delightful land he spreads
His orient beams, on herb, tree, fruit, and flower,
Glistering with dew; fragrant the fertile Earth
After soft showers, and sweet the coming-on
Of grateful Evening mild; then silent Night,
With this her solemn bird, and this fair Moon,
And these the gems of Heaven, her starry train;
But neither breath of Morn, when she ascends
With charm of earliest birds, nor rising Sun
On this delightful land, nor herb, fruit, flower,
Glistering with dew, nor fragrance after shower,
Nor grateful Evening mild, nor silent Night,
With this her solemn bird, nor walk by moon,
Or glittering starlight, without thee is sweet.
But wherefore all night long shine these? for whom
This glorious sight, when sleep hath shut all eyes?

William Shakespeare

Juliet: Come night! come, Romeo! come, thou day in night!
For thou wilt lie upon the wings of night,
Whiter than new snow on a raven's back.
Come, gentle night; come, loving, black-brow'd night,
Give me my Romeo: and, when he shall die,
Take him and cut him out in little stars,
And he will make the face of heaven so fine
That all the world will be in love with night,
And pay no worship to the garish sun.

SONNET XVIII

William Shakespeare

Shall I compare thee to a summer's day?
Thou art more lovely and more temperate:
Rough winds do shake the darling buds of May,
And summer's lease hath all too short a date:
Sometime too hot the eye of heaven shines,
And often is his gold complexion dimm'd:
And every fair from fair sometime declines,
By chance, or nature's changing course untrimm'd;
But thy eternal summer shall not fade,
Nor lose possession of that fair thou ow'st,
Nor shall death brag thou wander'st in his shade,
When in eternal lines to time thou grow'st;
    So long as men can breathe, or eyes can see,
    So long lives this, and this gives life to thee.

Read at the White House, April 30, 1963

SONNET XXIX
William Shakespeare

When, in disgrace with Fortune and men's eyes
I all alone beweep my outcast state,
And trouble deaf heaven with my bootless cries,
And look upon myself, and curse my fate,
Wishing me like to one more rich in hope,
Featured like him, like him with friends possest,
Desiring this man's art and that man's scope,
With what I most enjoy contented least;
Yet in these thoughts myself almost despising—
Haply I think on thee: and then my state,
Like to the Lark at break of day arising
From sullen earth, sings hymns at Heaven's gate;
    For thy sweet love rememb'red such wealth brings
    That then I scorn to change my state with Kings.

This poem was among my mother's suggestions to be read at the White House

SONNET CXVI
William Shakespeare

Let me not to the marriage of true minds
Admit impediments. Love is not love
Which alters when it alteration finds,
Or bends with the remover to remove:
O, no! it is an ever-fixed mark,
That looks on tempests and is never shaken;
It is the star to every wand'ring bark,
Whose worth's unknown, although his height be taken.
Love's not Time's fool, though rosy lips and cheeks
Within his bending sickle's compass come;
Love alters not with his brief hours and weeks,
But bears it out even to the edge of doom:
   If this be error and upon me proved,
    I never writ, nor no man ever loved.

THE BARGAIN
Sir Philip Sidney

My true love hath my heart, and I have his,
   By just exchange one for another given:
I hold his dear, and mine he cannot miss,
    There never was a better bargain driven:
      My true love hath my heart, and I have his.

His heart in me keeps him and me in one,
   My heart in him his thoughts and senses guides:
He loves my heart, for once it was his own,
    I cherish his because in me it bides:
      My true love hath my heart, and I have his.

THE PASSIONATE SHEPHERD TO HIS LOVE

Christopher Marlowe

Come live with me and be my Love,
And we will all the pleasures prove
That hills and valleys, dales and fields,
Or woods or steepy mountain yields.

And we will sit upon the rocks,
And see the shepherds feed their flocks
By shallow rivers, to whose falls
Melodious birds sing madrigals.

And I will make thee beds of roses
And a thousand fragrant posies;
A cap of flowers, and a kirtle
Embroider'd all with leaves of myrtle.

A gown made of the finest wool
Which from our pretty lambs we pull;
Fair-linèd slippers for the cold,
With buckles of the purest gold.

A belt of straw and ivy-buds
With coral clasps and amber studs:
And if these pleasures may thee move,
Come live with me and be my Love.

The shepherd swains shall dance and sing
For thy delight each May morning:
If these delights thy mind may move,
Then live with me and be my Love.

Read at the White House, April 30, 1963

HER REPLY
Sir Walter Raleigh

If all the world and love were young,
And truth in every shepherd's tongue,
These pretty pleasures might me move
To live with thee and be thy Love.

But Time drives flocks from field to fold;
When rivers rage and rocks grow cold;
And Philomel becometh dumb;
The rest complains of cares to come.

The flowers do fade, and wanton fields
To wayward Winter reckoning yields:
A honey tongue, a heart of gall,
Is fancy's spring, but sorrow's fall.

Thy gowns, thy shoes, thy beds of roses,
Thy cap, thy kirtle, and thy posies,
Soon break, soon wither—soon forgotten,
In folly ripe, in reason rotten.

Thy belt of straw and ivy-buds,
Thy coral clasps and amber studs,—
All these in me no means can move
To come to thee and be thy Love.

But could youth last, and love still breed,
Had joys no date, nor age no need,
Then these delights my mind might move
To live with thee and be thy Love.

This poem was one of my mother's suggestions to be read at the White House.

SHE WALKS IN BEAUTY

George Gordon, Lord Byron

She walks in beauty, like the night
   Of cloudless climes and starry skies,
And all that's best of dark and bright
   Meet in her aspect and her eyes,
Thus mellowed to that tender light
   Which heaven to gaudy day denies.

One shade the more, one ray the less,
   Had half impaired the nameless grace
Which waves in every raven tress
   Or softly lightens o'er her face,
Where thoughts serenely sweet express
   How pure, how dear their dwelling-place.

And on that cheek and o'er that brow
   So soft, so calm, yet eloquent,
The smiles that win, the tints that glow,
   But tell of days in goodness spent,—
A mind at peace with all below,
   A heart whose love is innocent.

DR. FAUSTUS

SCENE XIII

Christopher Marlowe

Faust: Was this the face that launched a thousand ships
Had burnt the topless towers of Ilium?
Sweet Helen, make me immortal with a kiss.
Her lips suck forth my soul; see where it flies!—
Come, Helen, come, give me my soul again.
Here will I dwell, for Heaven is in these lips,
And all is dross that is not Helena.
I will be Paris, and for love of thee,
Instead of Troy, shall Wittenberg be sack'd;
And I will combat with weak Menelaus,
And wear thy colours on my plumed crest;
Yea, I will wound Achilles in the heel,
And then return to Helen for a kiss.
Oh, thou art fairer than the evening air
Clad in the beauty of a thousand stars;
Brighter art thou than flaming Jupiter
When he appear'd to hapless Semele:
More lovely than the monarch of the sky
In wanton Arethusa's azured arms:
And none but thou shalt be my paramour.

This poem was one of my mother's suggestions to be read at the White House.

THE HILL
Rupert Brooke

Breathless, we flung us on the windy hill,
Laughed in the sun, and kissed the lovely grass.
You said, "Through glory and ecstasy we pass;
Wind, sun, and earth remain, the birds sing still,
When we are old, are old. . . ." "And when we die
All's over that is ours; and life burns on
Through other lovers, other lips," said I,
"Heart of my heart, our heaven is now, is won!"
"We are Earth's best, that learnt her lesson here.
Life is our cry. We have kept the faith!" we said;
"We shall go down with unreluctant tread
Rose-crowned into the darkness! . . ." Proud we were,
And laughed, that had such brave true things to say.
And then you suddenly cried, and turned away.

THE VASE OF PERFUME

Chang Wu-chien, translated by Gertrude L. Joerissen

If I open this flask of jade, in which is enclosed a wondrous perfume, its mysterious fragrance will overpower thee.

When I caress thee, O my vase of amber, do not breathe forth thy amorous thoughts.

WHEN A BEGGAR BEHOLDS YOU . . .

Anonymous (c. 324 A.D.), translated by Gertrude L. Joerissen

When the breeze inflates your two robes of silk
you look like a Goddess enveloped in clouds.

When you pass, the flowers of the mulberry tree
drink in your perfume. When you carry the lilacs
that you have gathered, they tremble with joy.

Bands of gold encircle your ankles, stones of blue
gleam in your girdle. A bird of jade has made its
nest in your hair. The roses of your cheeks mirror
themselves in the great pearls of your collar.

When you look at me I see the river Yuen flowing.
When you speak to me I hear the music of the
wind among the pines of my own country.

When a horseman meets you at dusk he thinks
it is already dawn, and brutally he brings his
horse to a standstill.

. . . When a beggar beholds you, he forgets his
hunger.

SOMEWHERE I HAVE NEVER TRAVELLED
E. E. Cummings

somewhere i have never travelled,gladly beyond
any experience,your eyes have their silence:
in your most frail gesture are things which enclose me,
or which i cannot touch because they are too near

your slightest look easily will unclose me
though i have closed myself as fingers,
you open always petal by petal myself as Spring opens
(touching skilfully, mysteriously)her first rose

or if your wish be to close me,i and
my life will shut very beautifully,suddenly,
as when the heart of this flower imagines
the snow carefully everywhere descending;

nothing which we are to perceive in this world equals
the power of your intense fragility:whose texture
compels me with the colour of its countries,
rendering death and forever with each breathing

(i do not know what it is about you that closes
and opens;only something in me understands
the voice of your eyes is deeper than all roses)
nobody,not even the rain, has such small hands

FOR C. K. AT HIS CHRISTENING
Daniel Lawrence Kelleher

We wish to the new child
A heart that can be beguiled
By a flower
That the wind lifts
As it passes.
If the storms break for him
May the trees shake for him
Their blossoms down.

In the night that he is troubled,
May a friend wake for him,
So that his time be doubled,
And at the end of all loving and love,
May the Man above
Give him a crown.

This poem was recited to my father by the Irish ambassador after John was born.

A PRAYER IN SPRING

Robert Frost

Oh, give us pleasure in the flowers today;
And give us not to think so far away
As the uncertain harvest; keep us here
All simply in the springing of the year.

Oh, give us pleasure in the orchard white,
Like nothing else by day, like ghosts by night;
And make us happy in the happy bees,
The swarm dilating round the perfect trees.

And make us happy in the darting bird
That suddenly above the bees is heard,
The meteor that thrusts in with needle bill,
And off a blossom in mid air stands still.

For this is love and nothing else is love,
The which it is reserved for God above
To sanctify to what far ends He will,
But which it only needs that we fulfill.

Read at the Dedication of John F. Kennedy Park, May 29, 1987.

Though I speak with the tongues of men and of angels, and have not charity, I am become *as* sounding brass, or a tinkling cymbal.

And though I have *the gift of* prophecy, and understand all mysteries, and all knowledge; and though I have all faith, so that I could remove mountains, and have not charity, I am nothing.

And though I bestow all my goods to feed *the poor*, and though I give my body to be burned, and have not charity, it profiteth me nothing.

Charity suffereth long, *and* is kind: charity envieth not; charity vaunteth not itself, is not puffed up.

Doth not behave itself unseemly, seeketh not her own, is not easily provoked, thinketh no evil;

Rejoiceth not in iniquity, but rejoiceth in the truth;

Beareth all things, believeth all things, hopeth all things, endureth all things.

Charity never falleth: but whether *there be* prophecies, they shall fail: whether *there be* tongues, they shall cease; whether *there be* knowledge, it shall vanish away.

For we know in part, and we prophesy in part.

But when that which is perfect is come, then that which is in part shall be done away.

When I was a child, I spake as a child, I understood as a child, I thought as a child: but when I became a man, I put away childish things.

For now we see through a glass, darkly; but then face to face: now I know in part; but then shall I know even as also I am known.

And now abideth faith, hope, charity, these three; but the greatest of these *is* charity.

REFLECTION

OCCASIONALLY, A POEM COMES to us almost like a message in a bottle we find while walking along the beach. When we are facing difficult times in our lives, when it may be hard to hear or see things clearly, a poem can carry thoughts from other times or places, from those who have faced similar challenges, and whose ability to articulate their experiences can bring moments of insight and calm.

These poems explore solitude, loss, and contemplation. They offer solace, wisdom, and hope. I have found that when a poem is passed from one person to another it deepens in meaning in an almost mystical way. There are poems in this section that meant something to my father, my mother, and my brother. Others came from cousins, friends, and from my husband and my children. By associating these works with people I love, each poem means that much more to me. I hope that by sharing them in this book, these poems will bring the same insight and joy to others.

To every *thing there is* a season, and a time to every purpose under the heaven:

A time to be born, and a time to die; a time to plant, and a time to pluck up *that which is* planted;

A time to kill, and a time to heal; a time to break down, and a time to build up;

A time to weep, and a time to laugh; a time to mourn, and a time to dance;

A time to cast away stones, and a time to gather stones together; a time to embrace, and a time to refrain from embracing;

A time to get, and a time to lose; a time to keep, and a time to cast away;

A time to rend, and a time to sew; a time to keep silence, and a time to speak;

A time to love, and a time to hate; a time of war, and a time of peace.

PRAYER FOR PEACE

St. Francis of Assisi

Lord, make me an instrument of Your Peace.
Where there is hatred, let me sow love,
Where there is injury, pardon,
Where there is doubt, faith,
Where there is despair, hope,
Where there is darkness, light,
    and where there is sadness, joy.

O Divine Master, grant that I may
    not so much seek to be consoled, as to console;
To be understood, as to understand;
To be loved, as to love;
For it is in giving that we receive;
It is in pardoning that we are pardoned;
And it is in dying that we are born to eternal life.

SONNET ON HIS BLINDNESS
John Milton

When I consider how my light is spent
   Ere half my days, in this dark world and wide,
   And that one talent, which is death to hide,
Lodged with me useless, though my soul more bent
To serve therewith my Maker, and present
   My true account, lest He, returning chide;
   "Doth God exact day labor, light denied?"
I fondly ask; but Patience, to prevent
   That murmur, soon replies, "God doth not need
      Either man's work, or His own gifts; who best
      Bear His mild yoke, they serve Him best.
         His state
Is kingly. Thousands at His bidding speed,
   And post o'er land and ocean without rest;
      They also serve who only stand and wait."

DEATH, BE NOT PROUD
John Donne

Death, be not proud, though some have called thee
Mighty and dreadful, for thou art not so:
For those whom thou think'st thou dost overthrow
Die not, poor Death; nor yet canst thou kill me.
From Rest and Sleep, which but thy picture be,
Much pleasure, then from thee much more must flow;
And soonest our best men with thee do go—
Rest of their bones and souls' delivery!
Thou'rt slave to fate, chance, kings, and desperate men,
And dost with poison, war, and sickness dwell;
And poppy or charms can make us sleep as well
And better than thy stroke. Why swell'st thou then?
   One short sleep past, we wake eternally,
    And Death shall be no more: Death, thou shalt die!

Read at the White House, April 30, 1963.

OZYMANDIAS

Percy Bysshe Shelley

I met a traveler from an antique land
Who said: Two vast and trunkless legs of stone
Stand in the desert. Near them, on the sand,
Half sunk, a shattered visage lies, whose frown
And wrinkled lip and sneer of cold command
Tell that its sculptor well those passions read
Which yet survive, stamped on these lifeless things,
The hand that mocked them and the heart that fed;
And on the pedestal these words appear:
"My name is Ozymandias, king of kings:
Look on my works, ye Mighty, and despair!"
Nothing beside remains. Round the decay
Of that colossal wreck, boundless and bare,
The lone and level sands stretch far away.

HIS PILGRIMAGE
Sir Walter Raleigh

Give me my scallop-shell of quiet,
   My staff of faith to walk upon,
My scrip of joy, immortal diet,
   My bottle of salvation,
My gown of glory, hope's true gage;
And thus I'll take my pilgrimage.

Blood must be my body's balmer;
   No other balm will there be given;
Whilst my soul, like quiet palmer,
   Travelleth towards the land of heaven;
Over the silver mountains,
Where spring the nectar fountains;
     There will I kiss
     The bowl of bliss;
     And drink mine everlasting fill
     Upon every milken hill.
     My soul will be a-dry before;
     But, after, it will thirst no more.

My mother suggested this poem be included in the White House evening of poetry.

Thou still unravish'd bride of quietness,
  Thou foster-child of Silence and slow Time,
Sylvan historian, who canst thus express
  A flowery tale more sweetly than our rhyme:
What leaf-fringed legend haunts about thy shape
  Of deities or mortals, or of both,
    In Tempe or the dales of Arcady?
  What men or gods are these? What maidens loth?
What mad pursuit? What struggle to escape?
  What pipes and timbrels? What wild ecstasy?

Heard melodies are sweet, but those unheard
  Are sweeter; therefore, ye soft pipes, play on;
Not to the sensual ear, but, more endear'd,
  Pipe to the spirit ditties of no tone:
Fair youth, beneath the trees, thou canst not leave
  Thy song, nor even can those trees be bare;
    Bold Lover, never, never canst thou kiss,
Though winning near the goal—yet, do not grieve;
    She cannot fade, though thou hast not thy bliss,
  For ever wilt thou love, and she be fair!

Ah, happy, happy boughs! that cannot shed
  Your leaves, nor ever bid the Spring adieu;
And, happy melodist, unwearièd,
  For ever piping songs for ever new;
More happy love! more happy, happy love!
  For ever warm and still to be enjoy'd,
    For ever panting and for ever young;

All breathing human passion far above,
   That leaves a heart high-sorrowful and cloy'd,
      A burning forehead, and a parching tongue.

Who are these coming to the sacrifice?
   To what green altar, O mysterious priest,
Lead'st thou that heifer lowing at the skies,
   And all her silken flanks with garlands drest?
What little town by river or sea-shore,
   Or mountain-built with peaceful citadel,
      Is emptied of its folk, this pious morn?
And, little town, thy streets for evermore
   Will silent be; and not a soul, to tell
      Why thou art desolate, can e'er return.

O Attic shape! fair attitude! with brede
   Of marble men and maidens overwrought,
With forest branches and the trodden weed;
   Thou, silent form! dost tease us out of thought
As doth eternity. Cold Pastoral!
   When old age shall this generation waste,
      Thou shalt remain, in midst of other woe
Than ours, a friend to man, to whom thou say'st,
'Beauty is truth, truth beauty,—that is all
      Ye know on earth, and all ye need to know.'

ANTIGONE

Sophocles

ODE I

Numberless are the world's wonders, but none
More wonderful than man; the stormgray sea
Yields to his prows, the huge crests bear him high;
Earth, holy and inexhaustible, is graven
With shining furrows where his plows have gone
Year after year, the timeless labor of stallions.

The lightboned birds and beasts that cling to cover,
The lithe fish lighting their reaches of dim water,
All are taken, tamed in the net of his mind;
The lion on the hill, the wild horse windy-maned,
Resign to him; and his blunt yoke has broken
The sultry shoulders of the mountain bull.

Words also, and thought as rapid as air,
He fashions to his good use; statecraft is his,
And his the skill that deflects the arrows of snow,
The spears of winter rain: from every wind
He has made himself secure—from all but one:
In the late wind of death he cannot stand.

O clear intelligence, force beyond all measure!
O fate of man, working both good and evil!
When the laws are kept, how proudly his city stands!
When the laws are broken, what of his city then?
Never may the anárchic man find rest at my hearth,
Never be it said that my thoughts are his thoughts.

AGAMEMNON

ACT I

Aeschylus

God, whose law it is that he who learns must suffer. And even in our sleep pain that cannot forget, falls drop by drop upon the heart, and in our own despite, against our will, comes wisdom to us by the awful grace of God.

Pindar

Their boon is life forever freed from toil.
No more to trouble earth or the sea waters
With their strong hands,
Laboring for the food that does not satisfy.
But with the favored of the gods they live
A life where there are no more tears.
Around those blessed isles soft sea winds breathe,
And golden flowers blaze upon the trees,
Upon the waters, too.

MAGPIES IN PICARDY

T. P. Cameron Wilson

The magpies in Picardy
Are more than I can tell.
They flicker down the dusty roads
And cast a magic spell
On the men who march through Picardy,
Through Picardy to hell.

(The blackbird flies with panic,
The swallow goes with light,
The finches move like ladies,
The owl floats by at night;
But the great and flashing magpie
He flies as artists might.)

A magpie in Picardy
Told me secret things—
Of the music in white feathers,
And the sunlight that sings
And dances in deep shadows—
He told me with his wings.

(The hawk is cruel and rigid,
He watches from a height;
The rook is slow and sombre,
The robin loves to fight;
But the great and flashing magpie
He flies as lovers might.)

The poet was killed in action in 1918.

He told me that in Picardy,
An age ago or more,
While all his fathers still were eggs,
These dusty highways bore
Brown, singing soldiers marching out
Through Picardy to war.

He said that still through chaos
Works on the ancient plan,
And two things have altered not
Since first the world began—
The beauty of the wild green earth
And the bravery of man.

(For the sparrow flies unthinking
And quarrels in his flight;
The heron trails his legs behind,
The lark goes out of sight;
But the great and flashing magpie
He flies as poets might.)

AFTERMATH

Siegfried Sassoon

Have you forgotten yet? . . .
For the world's events have rumbled on since those gagged
    days,
Like traffic checked while at the crossing of city-ways:
And the haunted gap in your mind has filled with thoughts
    that flow
Like clouds in the lit heaven of life; and you're a man reprieved
    to go,
Taking your peaceful share of Time, with joy to spare.
But the past is just the same—and War's a bloody game . . .
Have you forgotten yet? . . .
Look down, and swear by the slain of the War that you'll never forget.

Do you remember the dark months you held the sector at
    Mametz—
The nights you watched and wired and dug and piled sandbags
    on parapets?
Do you remember the rats; and the stench
Of corpses rotting in front of the front-line trench—
And dawn coming, dirty-white, and chill with a hopeless rain?
Do you ever stop and ask, 'Is it all going to happen again?'

Do you remember that hour of din before the attack—
And the anger, the blind compassion that seized and shook you
    then
As you peered at the doomed and haggard faces of your men?
Do you remember the stretcher-cases lurching back

With dying eyes and lolling heads—those ashen-grey
Masks of the lads who once were keen and kind and gay?

Have you forgotten yet? . . .
Look up, and swear by the green of the spring that you'll never forget.

THE SECOND COMING

William Butler Yeats

Turning and turning in the widening gyre
The falcon cannot hear the falconer;
Things fall apart; the centre cannot hold;
Mere anarchy is loosed upon the world,
The blood-dimmed tide is loosed, and everywhere
The ceremony of innocence is drowned;
The best lack all conviction, while the worst
Are full of passionate intensity.

Surely some revelation is at hand;
Surely the Second Coming is at hand.
The Second Coming! Hardly are those words out
When a vast image out of *Spiritus Mundi*
Troubles my sight: somewhere in sands of the desert
A shape with lion body and the head of a man
A gaze blank and pitiless as the sun,
Is moving its slow thighs, while all about it
Reel shadows of the indignant desert birds.
The darkness drops again; but now I know
That twenty centuries of stony sleep
Were vexed to nightmare by a rocking cradle,
And what rough beast, its hour come round at last,
Slouches towards Bethlehem to be born?

CHOOSE SOMETHING LIKE A STAR
Robert Frost

O Star (the fairest one in sight),
We grant your loftiness the right
To some obscurity of cloud—
It will not do to say of night,
Since dark is what brings out your light.
Some mystery becomes the proud.
But to be wholly taciturn
In your reserve is not allowed.
Say something to us we can learn
By heart and when alone repeat.
Say something! And it says, 'I burn.'
But say with what degree of heat.
Talk Fahrenheit, talk Centigrade.
Use language we can comprehend.
Tell us what elements you blend.
It gives us strangely little aid,
But does tell something in the end.
And steadfast as Keats' Eremite,
Not even stooping from its sphere,
It asks a little of us here.
It asks of us a certain height,
So when at times the mob is swayed
To carry praise or blame too far,
We may choose something like a star
To stay our minds on and be staid.

ONE ART

Elizabeth Bishop

The art of losing isn't hard to master;
so many things seem filled with the intent
to be lost that their loss is no disaster.

Lose something every day. Accept the fluster
of lost door keys, the hour badly spent.
The art of losing isn't hard to master.

Then practice losing farther, losing faster:
places, and names, and where it was you meant
to travel. None of these will bring disaster.

I lost my mother's watch. And look! my last, or
next-to-last, of three loved houses went.
The art of losing isn't hard to master.

I lost two cities, lovely ones. And, vaster,
some realms I owned, two rivers, a continent.
I miss them, but it wasn't a disaster.

—Even losing you (the joking voice, a gesture
I love) I shan't have lied. It's evident
the art of losing's not too hard to master
though it may look like (*Write* it!) like disaster.

THE NEGRO SPEAKS OF RIVERS
Langston Hughes

I've known rivers:
I've known rivers ancient as the world and older than the flow
    of human blood in human veins.

My soul has grown deep like the rivers.

I bathed in the Euphrates when dawns were young.
I built my hut near the Congo and it lulled me to sleep.
I looked upon the Nile and raised the pyramids above it.
I heard the singing of the Mississippi when Abe Lincoln went
    down to New Orleans, and I've seen its muddy bosom turn
    all golden in the sunset.

I've known rivers:
Ancient, dusky rivers.

My soul has grown deep like the rivers.

My daughter Rose chose this poem.

ACQUAINTED WITH THE NIGHT
Robert Frost

I have been one acquainted with the night.
I have walked out in rain—and back in rain.
I have outwalked the furthest city light.

I have looked down the saddest city lane.
I have passed by the watchman on his beat
And dropped my eyes, unwilling to explain.

I have stood still and stopped the sound of feet
When far away an interrupted cry
Came over houses from another street,

But not to call me back or say good-by;
And further still at an unearthly height,
One luminary clock against the sky

Proclaimed the time was neither wrong nor right.
I have been one acquainted with the night.

THE TRULY GREAT
Stephen Spender

I think continually of those who were truly great.
Who, from the womb, remembered the soul's history
Through corridors of light where the hours are suns,
Endless and singing. Whose lovely ambition
Was that their lips, still touched with fire,
Should tell of the Spirit, clothed from head to foot in song.
And who hoarded from the Spring branches
The desires falling across their bodies like blossoms.

What is precious, is never to forget
The essential delight of the blood drawn from ageless springs
Breaking through rocks in worlds before our earth.
Never to deny its pleasure in the morning simple light
Nor its grave evening demand for love.
Never to allow gradually the traffic to smother
With noise and fog, the flowering of the Spirit.

Near the snow, near the sun, in the highest fields,
See how these names are fêted by the waving grass
And by the streamers of white cloud
And whispers of wind in the listening sky.
The names of those who in their lives fought for life,
Who wore at their hearts the fire's centre.
Born of the sun, they travelled a short while toward the sun
And left the vivid air signed with their honour.

Read at the Dedication of the John F. Kennedy Library, October 20, 1979.

FOR A POET
Countee Cullen

To John Gaston Edgar

I have wrapped my dreams in a silken cloth,
And laid them away in a box of gold;
Where long will cling the lips of the moth,
I have wrapped my dreams in a silken cloth;
I hide no hate; I am not even wroth
Who found earth's breath so keen and cold;
I have wrapped my dreams in a silken cloth,
And laid them away in a box of gold.

HE WISHES FOR THE CLOTHS OF HEAVEN
William Butler Yeats

Had I the heavens' embroidered cloths,
Enwrought with golden and silver light,
The blue and the dim and the dark cloths
Of night and light and the half-light,
I would spread the cloths under your feet:
But I, being poor, have only my dreams;
I have spread my dreams under your feet;
Tread softly because you tread on my dreams.

My daughter Tatiana chose this poem.

And seeing the multitudes, he went up into a mountain: and when he was set, his disciples came unto him:

And he opened his mouth, and taught them, saying,

Blessed *are* the poor in spirit: for theirs is the kingdom of heaven.

Blessed *are* they that mourn: for they shall be comforted.

Blessed *are* the meek: for they shall inherit the earth.

Blessed *are* they which do hunger and thirst after righteousness: for they shall be filled.

Blessed *are* the merciful: for they shall obtain mercy.

Blessed *are* the pure in heart: for they shall see God.

Blessed *are* the peacemakers: for they shall be called the children of God.

Blessed *are* they which are persecuted for righteousness' sake: for theirs is the kingdom of heaven.

IN HER OWN WORDS

WHEN MY MOTHER WAS WORKING as a literary editor, she wrote the following as part of an anthology called *Books I Read When I Was Young* published by the National Council of Teachers of English.

My mother felt fortunate to have had English teachers who changed her life. When she spoke about the poetry evening at the White House, she was especially proud that she had been able to find and invite her high school English teacher, who had first taught her to love Shakespeare.

Although I know my mother would have felt slightly embarrassed to have her own poems included with the ones in this book that she so admired, they have meant a lot to our family, and I wanted to share them. She allowed them to be published during her life, and they reveal a bit about her in her own words. Though writing poetry can seem difficult, I hope these poems will also encourage readers to write poetry of their own.

Read for escape, read for adventure, read for romance, but read the great writers. You will find to your delight that they are easier and more joy to read than the second-rate ones. They touch your imagination and your deepest yearnings, and when your imagination is stirred it can lead you down paths you never dreamed you would travel. If you read great language you will develop, without your realizing it, an appreciation of excellence that can shape your life.

Read Edgar Allan Poe, Jack London, Jules Verne, Ernest Hemingway. And read poetry—in whatever anthology your school gives you. Rhythm is what should first seize you when you read poetry. Do you know "Tarantella" by Hilaire Belloc? Read Countee Cullen, e.e. cummings, Emily Dickinson, Siegfried Sassoon. Do you know "The Fog" by Carl Sandburg? It is modelled on the Japanese haiku which is only allowed to be seventeen syllables long and doesn't have to rhyme. You could try to write a poem like that.

If you read, you may want to write. Great painters learned to paint by copying Old Masters in museums. You can learn to write by trying to copy the writers you like. Writing helps you to express your deepest feelings. Once you can express yourself you can tell the world what you want from it or how you would like to change it. All the changes in the world, for good or evil, were first brought about by words.

—1980

SEA JOY

Jacqueline Bouvier

When I go down by the sandy shore
I can think of nothing I want more
Than to live by the booming blue sea
As the seagulls flutter round about me

I can run about—when the tide is out
With the wind and the sand and the sea all about
And the seagulls are swirling and diving for fish
Oh—to live by the sea is my only wish.

—*1939*

THOUGHTS
Jacqueline Bouvier

I love the Autumn,
And yet I cannot say
All the thoughts and things
That make one feel this way.

I love walking on the angry shore,
To watch the angry sea;
Where summer people were before,
But now there's only me.

I love wood fires at night
That have a ruddy glow.
I stare at the flames
And think of long ago.

I love the feeling down inside me
That says to run away
To come and be a gypsy
And laugh the gypsy way.

The tangy taste of apples,
The snowy mist at morn,
The wanderlust inside you
When you hear the huntsman's horn.

Nostalgia—that's the Autumn,
Dreaming through September
Just a million lovely things
I always will remember.

—1943

MEANWHILE IN MASSACHUSETTS
Jacqueline Bouvier Kennedy

Meanwhile in Massachusetts Jack Kennedy dreamed

Walking the shore by the Cape Cod Sea
Of all the things he was going to be.

He breathed in the tang of the New England fall
And back in his mind he pictured it all,
The burnished New England countryside
Names that a patriot says with pride
Concord and Lexington, Bunker Hill
Plymouth and Falmouth and Marstons Mill
Winthrop and Salem, Lowell, Revere
Quincy and Cambridge, Louisburg Square.
This was his heritage—this his share
Of dreams that a young man harks in the air.
The past reached out and tracked him now

He would heed that touch; he didn't know how.
Part he must serve, a part he must lead
Both were his calling, both were his need.

Part he was of New England stock
As stubborn, close guarded as Plymouth Rock
He thought with his feet most firm on the ground
But his heart and his dreams were not earthbound
He would call New England his place and his creed
But part he was of an alien breed
Of a breed that had laughed on Irish hills
And heard the voices in Irish rills.

The lilt of that green land danced in his blood
Tara, Killarney, a magical flood
That surged in the depth of his too proud heart

And spiked the punch of New England so tart
Men would call him thoughtful, sincere
They would not see through to the Last Cavalier.

He turned on the beach and looked toward his house.

On a green lawn his white house stands
And the wind blows the sea grass low on the sands
There his brothers and sisters have laughed and played
And thrown themselves to rest in the shade.
The lights glowed inside, soon supper would ring
And he would go home where his father was King.
But now he was here with the wind and the sea
And all the things he was going to be.

> He would build empires
> And he would have sons
> Others would fall
> Where the current runs
>
> He would find love
> He would never find peace
> For he must go seeking
> The Golden Fleece
>
> All of the things he was going to be
> All of the things in the wind and the sea.

—October 1953

(Inspired by "John Brown's Body" by Stephen Vincent Benét)

"Of Mere Being" by Wallace Stevens. From *Opus Posthumous* by Wallace Stevens, edited by Samuel French Morse, copyright © by Elsie Stevens and Holly Stevens. Used by permission of Alfred A. Knopf, a division of Random House, Inc.

"Brown River, Smile" by Jean Toomer. Reprinted with permission of the Yale Collection of American Literature and Beinecke Rare Book and Manuscript Library, Yale University.

"Dogs and Weather" by Winifred Welles. Printed with permission of the Winifred Welles Estate, reprinted from *Skipping Along Alone* by Winifred Welles, published by MacMillan. Reprinted with the permission of Gail Shearer.

"The Red Wheelbarrow" by William Carlos Williams, from *Collected Poems: 1909–1939, Volume 1,* copyright © 1938 by New Directions Publishing Corp. Reprinted by permission of New Directions Publishing Corp.

"The Second Coming," "He Wishes for the Cloths of Heaven," "The Song of Wandering Aengus," "The Dawn," "The Lake Isle of Innisfree," "Sailing to Byzantium" by William Butler Yeats. Reprinted with the permission of Scribner, a Division of Simon & Schuster, Inc., from *The Collected Poems of W. B. Yeats: Revised 2nd Edition* by Richard J. Finneran. (New York: Scribner, 1996).

PHOTO CREDITS

Photograph appearing on page iii © John F. Kennedy Library, Boston
Photograph appearing on page xi © Brooks Kraft/Gamma
Photograph appearing on page 1 © Jacques Lowe
Photograph appearing on page 3 © George Silk/Timepix
Photograph appearing on page 29 © John F. Kennedy Library, Boston
Photograph appearing on page 31 © Collection of Caroline Kennedy